Easy
Low Carb Cooking

Over 150 delicious recipes for everyday use

Patricia Haakonson

Foreword by Dr. Michael E. Platt

All nutrition information calculated using the NutriBase 2000 Personal Plus software, by CyberSoft, Inc.
Revised edition June 2002

Printed and bound in Victoria, British Columbia, Canada
Book design, typesetting:
Vivencia Resources Group
www.members.shaw.ca/vrg
Cover design: Roy Diment, VRG
Cover photo: Destrube Photography

National Library of Canada Cataloguing in Publication Data

Haakonson, Patricia, 1950-
     Easy low carb cooking / Patricia Haakonson.

Previously published under title: Everyday low carb cooking.
ISBN 1-55369-497-X

     1. Low-carbohydrate diet—Recipes.   I. Title.   II. Title:
Everyday low carb cooking.

RM237.73.H32 2002   641.5'638   C2002-901931-1

TRAFFORD

This book was published *on-demand* in cooperation with Trafford Publishing.
On-demand publishing is a unique process and service of making a book available for retail sale to the public taking advantage of on-demand manufacturing and Internet marketing.
On-demand publishing includes promotions, retail sales, manufacturing, order fulfilment, accounting and collecting royalties on behalf of the author.

Suite 6E, 2333 Government St., Victoria, B.C. V8T 4P4, CANADA
Phone	250-383-6864	Toll-free	1-888-232-4444 (Canada & US)
Fax	250-383-6804	E-mail	sales@trafford.com
Web site	www.trafford.com	TRAFFORD PUBLISHING IS A DIVISION OF TRAFFORD HOLDINGS LTD.
Trafford Catalogue #02-0310		www.trafford.com/robots/02-0310.html	

10   9   8   7   6   5   4   3

Low Carb Recipes

Salads

Vegetables

Poultry

Poultry cont.

Fish

Meats

Desserts

FOREWORD

By Michael E. Platt, M.D.
Board Certified, Internal Medicine

For many years, people struggling to lose weight were basically all given the same advice: diet, exercise and watch your fat intake. Unfortunately, the incorporation of this approach to weight loss has led to an epidemic of obesity because for 99% of the population it just won't work.

My name is Michael E. Platt, M.D. A large part of my clinical career has been devoted exclusively to the metabolic approach to weight control – i.e. the underlying reason why a person is creating and holding on to fat. Most of my patients have been over-producers of insulin, the hormone that creates fat around the middle. Other patients have had problems related to other hormones, or taking medications affecting their metabolism (i.e. beta blockers, anti-depressants, estrogen preparations etc.). And there was the rare patient whose only problem was incorrect eating habits.

Restriction of carbohydrates for weight loss is enjoying a resurgence of popularity. It is not a new concept as it's been around for over 150 years. What's unique about it is that it can be utilized for anyone who wants to lose weight since it automatically reduces insulin levels, the main culprit for creating and maintaining fat.

Please keep in mind that not all low-carb approaches to weight loss are the same. People that are true over-producers of insulin (i.e. those who nod off between 3 and 4 p.m. or while driving in a car) cannot succeed with "reward meal" approaches, diets allowing yams or unlimited protein etc. The benefit of this particular low-carb cookbook is that it is a truly generic approach, suitable for anyone desiring to lose weight by burning fat. This kind of meal plan is ideal for people with diabetes, but will require an adjustment of medications downward. Adherence to the meal plans in this book will cause a decrease in triglyceride and cholesterol levels and can also lower blood pressure because of a decrease in insulin levels.

INTRODUCTION

It is now more than two years since I was introduced to the concept of a low carbohydrate diet. Dr. Michael Platt, of Palm Desert California, suggested I try a low carb approach to food as a weight loss program. Dr. Platt's Metabolic Solutions ® is a formula similar to the more widely known Dr. Atkins' (Low Carbohydrate) Diet. There are many diets which employ the same basic principles of a low carbohydrate eating program, including the Protein Power Lifeplan, the Sugar Busters Diet, the Carbohydrate Addict's Diet, and The Zone.

The basic principle upon which any low carbohydrate diet is based is simple. The body, in order to create energy, will burn either fat or sugar for fuel. By reducing the amount of carbohydrates we ingest (which the body metabolizes to sugar for energy conversion), we force the body to burn fat for energy. I am told that it takes three days of low carbohydrate eating before the body converts to fat burning for energy. Then, if we consume less fat than we need to maintain our activity level, we will actually start to burn the fat that our bodies have stored over the years. During maintenance we can increase the amount of carbohydrates because we are no longer concerned with burning stored fat. As with any weight loss or weight management program, moderate exercise on a regular basis will improve overall health and well being.

I was skeptical about this approach to eating and weight loss, and worried that I would not be able to stick to the stringent requirement to give up my beloved breads, bagels, potatoes and pasta. I had adopted a diet that was almost exclusively carbohydrate in my efforts to reduce my fat intake. What I unwittingly did was sabotage my body without knowing it. I was overproducing insulin. This resulted in loss of energy, and periods of lethargy induced by insulin highs and low blood sugar.

How I managed to stick to my new eating regime for the first few days was to promise myself everyday that if I stuck to the diet today, I could "cheat" and have a bagel tomorrow. Then I would get up the next day and promise myself the same thing, all over again. I was surprised to discover that after the first two weeks or so, the cravings for carbohydrate loaded foods completely disappeared.

Over the next 12 weeks I followed Dr. Platt's recommendations and kept my carbohydrate intake below 30 grams a day. It turned out to be a lot easier than I anticipated! To my delight I lost a total of 40 pounds which I have successfully kept off for more than two years. I have progressed to a maintenance level of carbohydrate intake and plan to maintain this weight in the future.

I will never go back to my old eating habits. I made this decision because I feel so much healthier than I have in years. This lifestyle change has made it easy to maintain the weight loss. I have seemingly endless amounts of energy, with no "low" spots during the day. An added bonus for me is that a bowel disease (called colitis) that I have battled for over 30 years has all but disappeared. I have not had any of the debilitating symptoms that I used to suffer, since starting the low carbohydrate approach to eating.

I made a decision to maintain a low carbohydrate lifestyle. This is the approach to food that allows me to maintain an optimum level of health and energy as well as an optimum weight. Once this decision was made, I determined I needed to broaden the scope of recipes I was using. I have been interested in cooking and baking for many years, having learned the basics at a very early age from my mother. I have taken many culinary courses over the years and have picked up pointers from family and friends along the way.

When I decided to search out new and interesting recipes that met the low carbohydrate standard, I was very disappointed. My local bookstore did a search and found only two books in print. I ordered one, but was not happy with the recipes it contained, particularly the dessert section. I still think that dinner is not complete without a dessert. I am content to have sugar free jello on most nights to adhere to a low carbohydrate regime, but not every night.

As part of my research, I went to the Internet where a search resulted in no matches. I lamented the lack of resources to family and friends and set about to create my own low carbohydrate recipes. This became a fulfilling creative outlet, as I developed new recipes and thought about how to modify some old standards, to adhere to a low carbohydrate approach. It was one of my family members that mentioned I ought to consider putting my recipes together in a cookbook. This is the result.

I hope that you will enjoy this collection of low carbohydrate recipes. I have attempted to make the directions easy to follow. I have also tried to ensure the ingredients are everyday things that you will find in most kitchens. (One low carbohydrate cookbook used ingredients like soy flour and tofu flour, as well as a secret baking "mix" which could be ordered by phoning a 1-800 number!)

In food preparation we generally derive flavor from using either sugar or fat. Because low carbohydrate diets limit the amount of sugar, much of our flavor comes from fat. So you will see recipes in this cookbook that use heavy cream, bacon fat and butter to provide flavor. These ingredients have been limited to allow you to maintain what I believe is a healthy balance of nutrients. I have also used spices and fresh herbs to enhance flavor and presentation of many dishes contained within these pages.

For every recipe in this cookbook you will find Nutritional Information provided on a per serving basis. Some low carbohydrate cookbooks provide the number of grams of carbohydrate for each serving without any idea of the calories or fat content. While I don't count calories, I do like to be able to balance my intake. If I have one menu item which is highly caloric, the other items on the menu will be less so, to balance my daily intake. This just makes common sense to me. I am not interested in the grams of carbohydrate in a dish, in isolation from other considerations. All nutritional information was developed using the NutriBase 2000 Personal Plus software from Cybersoft Inc. out of Phoenix, Arizona. Every effort has been made to ensure the accuracy of the nutrition information.

If you wish to lose weight, I recommend that you visit your family doctor to make sure a low carbohydrate approach to eating is appropriate for you. It is not my intention to convince readers that low carbohydrate eating is the only way to go. My intention is to provide tools to those that have already been converted to this approach to eating.

My second book, *Easy Low Carb Living*, was designed to provide readers with a better understanding of the low carb mechanism and an outline of how to adopt a low carb lifestyle. This book, co-authored with my physician husband, Harv Haakonson, also provides a full week of menu planning for weight loss, a week of menu planning for maintenance, and some menu ideas for entertaining. All of the menu planning is done using recipes from this cookbook. In addition, readers will find reviews of the popular low carb diets, a personal food diary and an easy carbohydrate counter to facilitate learning to eat the low carb way.

Because low carbohydrate cooking and low carbohydrate living may be new to some readers, I have included a section on Helpful Hints to guide you through the initial tough spots. These include suggestions for eating out in restaurants, eating out at friends, feeding the rest of the family, how to shop, how to manage at a movie or adjust a favorite recipe of your own. I hope that you will enjoy experimenting with these concepts and ideas. I would be happy to hear from readers who have suggestions for additions, or recipes that they would like to see in any future edition. If you have any questions, please contact me at my website, www.lowcarbliving.ca.

HELPFUL HINTS

*T*his section of the cookbook provides some tips on living with a low carbohydrate meal plan. It took me some months to figure out that these precautions and a little planning could make life a lot easier. I hope that they will do the same for you. If you are interested in more detailed suggestions for living a low carbohydrate lifestyle, you might want to read my second book, *Easy Low Carb Living*.

∼ SNACKS ∼

Always have low carbohydrate snacks readily at hand. There are many kinds of snacks that qualify and it is simply a matter of choosing the ones that you like. If you do this you will never get caught in a meeting/ shopping/ on a golf course or visiting with friends and be without something to quiet your hunger pangs. I find it convenient to carry low carbohydrate protein bars with me. There are many of these available, including the Dr. Atkins' "Advantage" bar and "Ultimate Lo Carb Bar", by Biochem® Sport & Fitness Systems. Other new items include low carb bars and drinks, as well as special vitamin supplements by a company called CarbSolutions. Recent information causes me to caution readers in the use of these bars. There is new evidence that the nutrition information may be incorrect on the label, and these bars may have more carbohydrates than advertised. My new book *Easy Low Carb Living* contains full details concerning recent research on these bars. These products can be found in Health Food Stores, Drugstores, and Nutrition Stores. New products are cropping up all over the place. That's great news for us – more choice and easier access. Other easy to carry snacks include hard boiled eggs, cheese strings or hard cheese, and nuts.

∼ EATING OUT IN RESTAURANTS ∼

It is becoming easier to eat out in restaurants and have your dietary restrictions met. In order to keep customers happy and increase return business, many restaurants are very willing to accommodate your special requests. I have asked for burgers without the bun and a small side salad, with great success. If eating a dinner out, I often start with a green salad and avoid any rolls or garlic bread. I usually request a vinaigrette dressing, but there are many dressings which are low in carbohydrates. I always ask to have the potato or rice removed from my plate, and additional vegetables substituted. I have never had my request denied at any restaurant – whether fast food or expensive dining. At one establishment, when I finished ordering, the waitress said with a big smile, "I know what diet you're on!" If other members of my party order desserts, I order herb tea, to keep my hands busy and have something hot and tasty to drink. These strategies have enabled me to enjoy many meals in restaurants without either feeling deprived or "cheating" on my food plan.

∼ EATING OUT AT FRIENDS' HOMES ∼

When friends hear that you are following a special diet, they may hesitate to have you over for meals, fearing that their choices will be limited or preparation difficult. I always mention to friends that other than a pasta dish, I will eat anything but the potato or rice they may serve. I decline any roll or bread, and ask for small portions of any dessert. If my host is serving carrots or corn (very high in carbohydrates) as the main vegetable, I will eat a small portion and watch my intake the following day. All this makes the occasion stress free and fun for both the host and myself. I also often carry a small bottle of club soda or Perrier with me in case the host doesn't have any carbonated water. I leave it in the car initially, and only bring it in if necessary.

~ FEEDING THE REST OF THE FAMILY ~

My husband was not on a low carbohydrate plan when I started mine. I had to develop some strategies to keep him happy without tempting myself too much. What I did was prepare potatoes for him using a method that I don't like (baked in the microwave or plain boiled). I also prepared rice for him (which I don't particularly like) so I was not tempted. I gave him extra portions of vegetable and sometimes a roll or bread with his dinner. I bought ice cream and cookies in flavors that I don't like so they were available for him. It gets easier and easier to resist these sorts of foods. And, he has now also decided to adopt a low carb meal plan – entirely his choice.

~ TREATS ~

I still like sweets, and have not completely gotten rid of my sweet tooth. I have devised a number of relatively low carbohydrate treats that I allow myself once in a while. Some of my standard treats include sugar free gum and sugar free mints. You must be careful to read the labels of various manufacturers to determine the carbohydrate content, and watch how many you eat.

I discovered that a local chocolate maker (Purdy's of Victoria, BC) produces a "no sugar added" chocolate truffle aimed at the diabetic community. Their nutrition information states there are 4 grams of carbohydrate in each truffle, and I allow myself just one of these delicious treats every once in a while.

I haunt the diabetic aisles in the grocery store looking for sugar free candies and other small treats to help satisfy my sweet tooth. I have found many little things I keep around for when I can no longer resist.

It is interesting to note that I read somewhere that eating small treats like this, or adding flour in small amounts to recipes would instantly bring back all the cravings for carbohydrates that we worked so hard to get over. This has not been my experience. I think all things in moderation works best, and I never allow myself to feast on any of these sweets – they are reserved for the occasional special treat.

~ GOING TO THE MOVIES ~

I hate to admit it, but I actually bring small amounts of snack foods with me to the movies, since I can no longer enjoy popcorn or regular soft drinks. I usually choose to bring a small bag of nuts and some sugar free gum or mints. I buy bottled water or an occasional diet soft drink from the concession stand, partly to assuage my conscience. Please be aware that most diet drinks contain aspartame, and some people react adversely to this sugar substitute.

~ PLANNING ~

Perhaps the single most helpful thing is to plan your meals and meal preparation so that you are not caught short. I cannot rush home anymore at noon, and make myself a quick peanut butter sandwich – it just doesn't work. I almost always cook more than I need of certain items, so I have extras left over in the fridge to use for lunches or snacks. I usually have cooked chicken breasts in the fridge that I can have cold or hot with a salad or coleslaw as a quick and easy lunch. When I make a green salad or cole-slaw, I make enough for a couple of days and keep the additional portions in covered plastic containers in the fridge. (I'm lazy and can't be bothered to take a lot of time over lunch on a daily ba-sis.) This type of planning in advance makes preparation quick and easy. I never shop for food without a list and I don't buy anything that is not on my list. I don't even walk down the cookie aisle, unless looking for something for my husband. Even then, I always look for ones that I don't like. (Yes, I can be weak willed.)

~ READ LABELS ~

It is important to read labels very carefully. I found, especially at the beginning, that eating low carb was not intuitive. After years of trying to eat low fat, and buying reduced fat products, all of a sudden I discovered that I wanted to buy regular mayonnaise or salad dressing. Reduced fat products usually contain increased amounts of sugar for flavor, to make up for the missing fat. What this does is increase the carbohydrate content. I recommend you become one of those people who stand in the aisles at the grocery store and read all the labels.

∽ DRINKS ∽

On a weight loss program, it is recommended that you do not drink alcohol. It is also recommended that you use decaffeinated coffee (caffeine stimulates insulin production in the body). You can drink diet soda or Crystal Light (a powder that you add to water to make fruit-like drinks). My personal favorite is Fresca, which contains 0 calories and 0 carbs. I want to caution you about aspartame, which is found in most diet drinks, including Crystal Light. Many people react adversely to this sugar substitute and suffer from headaches and other symptoms after eating or drinking anything that contains aspartame. You can make an informed decision about your own tolerance level. You should always drink lots of water, especially during a weight loss plan. I particularly like carbonated water as a refreshing drink, and I often add a wedge of lemon or lime to provide a bit of flavor.

∽ STICKING TO IT ∽

I have lost my desire for the breads and pastas that I used to eat on a frequent basis. I am very motivated to stay on a low carbohydrate plan because of how well I feel. I have maintained my ideal weight for over two years. I do allow myself the occasional carbohydrate intense treat. (I had a chocolate mousse for dessert on my 50th Birthday!) If I have something high in carbohydrates, I carefully watch my intake for the balance of the week. I still record my daily food intake and weigh myself once a week to keep on top of things.

The record keeping is easy once you get in the habit. I highly recommend tracking what you eat, until you are thoroughly familiar with a low carb meal plan. If there is a small weight gain, it is relatively easy to go back and review what you had to eat. You can then decide what you need to change in the coming week, to lose the small gain and ensure that it doesn't happen again. We have provided a personal food diary and a carbohydrate counter in our new book, *Easy Low Carb Living*. We have also provided a food diary on our website, www.lowcarbliving.ca, that can be downloaded and printed to help you track your carb consumption.

LOW CARB COOKING TIPS

～ PREPARATION ～

As with any other kind of cooking, it is best to be prepared when you are trying a new recipe. Read through the recipe before starting to ensure that you have all the ingredients on hand, as well as the proper tools and equipment. I also like to make sure that my kitchen is clean and uncluttered before beginning.

～ ORGANIZATION ～

It is easy to follow even a complicated recipe (there aren't many in this cookbook), by preparing the necessary ingredients before starting to cook. I measure and prepare all ingredients and put them in small dishes or containers so that they are at my fingertips when the recipe calls for them.

～ FRESH HERBS ～

I love to grow fresh herbs in pots just outside my kitchen. It doesn't take a lot of space or time, and it makes a wonderful difference in the taste, smell and appearance of most dishes. It is somehow very satisfying to go out and snip a few herbs as I get ready to prepare a meal. I find that there is something relaxing and soothing about working with fragrant herbs. The ones that I always grow are flat leaf parsley and regular parsley, mint, thyme, lemon thyme, rosemary, dill, and chives. If you are unable or not inclined to grow fresh herbs, most markets and grocery stores sell them in the fresh produce section.

～ FINE HERBS ～

You will notice that I use a dried herb that is called Fine Herbs (or sometimes found with the French spelling of *Fines Herbes*) in a number of recipes. This is a mix of dried herbs associated with French cuisine. I really like the flavor, especially when I am not using fresh herbs. This blend of herbs is manufactured by many different spice companies. I have found them on the shelf of every grocery store where I shop.

～ PRESENTATION ～

The presentation of a dish is important. I think this is especially true when people worry that the cuisine is in some way lacking (as someone might when starting to eat low carb). There are many things that can be done to enhance the presentation of a dish. I have included a number of simple ideas in the text of recipes, like adding a sprig of mint or dill as garnish for certain dishes. Other ideas to consider include using edible flowers (nasturtium or pansy) to garnish a salad or dessert. Attention to presentation will immediately enhance the look of a dish and delight the senses.

～ IMAGINATION ～

Once you become comfortable with low carb cooking, you can begin to experiment to suit your own tastes. Change the herbs in a sauce or substitute a different vegetable in a salad or soup. A little bit of imagination goes a long way. Keep in mind which ingredients you want to avoid. It is not as easy to experiment with baking, which is a bit like chemistry where all the ingredients must be exact to achieve the desired results.

∿ EQUIPMENT ∿

It is easiest to prepare tasty meals if you have the right equipment. Tools don't have to be the top of the line, but they must get the job done. One small piece of equipment that I recommend is a "rasp" or "zester" to get the zest from citrus fruits. These are not expensive. They are made with very sharp, small cutting surfaces especially designed to take only the colored zest from a lemon, lime or orange. They make the job so much easier than trying to work with a regular grater.

∿ LEMONS & LIMES ∿

I always have lots of fresh lemons and limes in the fridge. I use them for everything – a twist or wedge in a glass of water to make it more refreshing, as dressing for some cucumber fingers or other vegetable for a quick snack, or to add some zip to sauces or a bare salad.

∿ SUGAR SUBSTITUTES ∿

There are many sugar substitutes available on the market these days. I prefer Splenda™. This low carb sweetner does not change flavor or texture when baking, which was the primary concern to me. Splenda™ does not contain aspartame, and it carries no known health risk. It is easy to use and available widely. I generally buy the small packets for convenience. The Splenda™ in packets is a concentrated form, equivalent to two teaspoons of sugar. It can also be purchased in granular form, which only requires that you measure the amount needed. The granular form is not concentrated, and may be used in equivalent measure to sugar. If you are following recipes in this cookbook and can only find the granular form, use two teaspoons for every packet in the recipe.

~ A WORD ABOUT FATS ~

You might notice some of the recipes contain more fat than you have used in recent years. There are many reasons for this. Fats provide flavor and contribute to a feeling of satiation. Fats are essential for cell development and to aid in the digestion of certain nutrients. The most important consideration when eating fat is to ensure it is one of the "good" fats. I have used olive oil, one of the "good" unsaturated fats, almost exclusively in my recipe development. You will not find margarine, with its hydrogenated ("bad") fats anywhere in this cookbook. In addition, the fat content in many of the chicken, fish and meat recipes comes from olive oil used in a marinade. While the olive oil must be included in the nutrition calculation, it is important to note that much of it stays behind in the dish when the food item is cooked. This means the fat grams in the nutrition box will be slightly elevated, compared to actual consumption.

~ ADJUSTING YOUR FAMILY FAVORITES ~

If you want to experiment with adjusting favorite recipes your family doesn't want to give up, you need to try to eliminate or drastically reduce any flour in the recipe. Other ingredients to keep to a minimum are cornstarch or other thickener. Also eliminate things like rice, potato and bread, including croutons, and breadcrumbs. This may take some time to experiment and find out what works for the individual recipe. In some cases, you can change other ingredients to help make up for the lack of flour. For example, using light or heavy cream in a sauce rather than milk will allow you to reduce the need for flour. Sometimes you can add an egg or some cheese to make up for bread in a recipe. It just takes some time and a little experimentation. I welcome your recipe ideas at our website, www.lowcarbliving.ca .

APPETIZERS

Avocado Dip

½ cup sour cream

½ cup mayonnaise

1 small ripe avocado

2 green onions, chopped

⅓ cup fresh chopped parsley

2 tablespoons fresh lemon juice

1 clove garlic, minced

1 tablespoon fresh chopped thyme

Nutrition Information Per Serving	
Calories	28.22
Protein	0.13 g.
Carbs	0.81 g.
Fat	2.79 g.

- ❀ Peel avocado and remove pit. Cut into small pieces.
- ❀ Put all ingredients into a blender or food processor and process until smooth.
- ❀ Place dip in a small bowl, cover with plastic wrap and refrigerate for 2-3 hours. Just before serving garnish with some fresh chopped parsley.
- ❀ Serve with slices of cucumber, zucchini or small crackers.
- ❀ Makes approximately 2 cups.

Note: This dip is a beautiful green with dark flecks from the fresh herbs. It tastes wonderful and is so easy to make. The nutrition calculation is based on 50 servings.

Deviled Eggs with Chives

6 eggs

2 tablespoons sour cream

2 tablespoons mayonnaise

2 teaspoons fresh lemon juice

2 teaspoons fresh chopped chives

1 teaspoon Dijon mustard

pinch of paprika

Nutrition Information Per Serving	
Calories	56.07
Protein	3.22 g.
Carbs	0.58 g.
Fat	4.53 g.

※ Place eggs in a saucepan with enough water to cover them. Bring water to a boil and cook for 10 minutes. Remove eggs from hot water and wash with cold water until eggs are cool. Refrigerate for 30 minutes to cool completely.

※ Crack the egg shells all around and peel shells. Cut eggs in half lengthwise.

※ Remove yolks carefully and place whites on serving dish.

※ In a small bowl crush yolks with a fork. Add all remaining ingredients except paprika and whisk until smooth.

※ Spoon yolk mixture into the hollow whites and swirl the tops. Sprinkle with a dash of paprika to add color.

※ Makes 12 servings.

Curried Crab

¾ cup chopped crabmeat

½ cup finely chopped celery

½ cup real mayonnaise

2 tablespoons chopped green onion

1 tablespoon dried parsley

1 teaspoon curry powder

½ teaspoon dried mustard

⅛ teaspoon cayenne pepper

freshly ground pepper & salt to taste

small English cucumber, sliced

1 teaspoon freshly minced parsley, to garnish

Nutrition Information Per Serving	
Calories	21.17
Protein	0.88 g.
Carbs	0.13 g.
Fat	1.90 g.

❀ Put all ingredients, except the cucumber, in medium bowl and mix well. The curried crabmeat will keep well in the fridge for up to a full day.

❀ Place a small amount of crabmeat on each cucumber slice. (You may also use small wheat crackers, although this will dramatically increase the carbohydrates.)

❀ Place on serving platter, and garnish with freshly minced parsley.

❀ Makes approximately 48 pieces.

Mushrooms Stuffed with Asparagus Puree

½ lb. fresh asparagus (about 12 spears)

1 tablespoon sour cream

½ teaspoon heavy cream

1 tablespoon olive oil

2 cloves garlic, finely minced

2 tablespoons fresh chopped parsley

1 tablespoon grated cheese (cheddar or parmesan)

36 medium sized fresh mushrooms

Nutrition Information Per Serving	
Calories	12.74
Protein	0.74 g.
Carbs	1.06 g.
Fat	0.69 g.

- Clean mushrooms with a small brush or paper towel, and remove stems. Set aside.
- Preheat oven to 375°.
- Cut off the tips of the asparagus and chop roughly, set aside. Cut the spears into 2" pieces and cook in boiling water until soft, about 5 minutes. Drain well. Add cooked spears, sour cream and heavy cream to food processor and process until smooth. Add salt and fresh ground pepper to taste.
- In a small frying pan, heat olive oil and add garlic and asparagus tops. Sauté for 2-3 minutes and then add the parsley. Continue cooking for one minute longer.
- Grease the bottom of a glass oven-proof dish with butter. Place the mushroom caps evenly in the dish.
- Fill each mushroom cap with the asparagus puree. Add a small amount of the garlic and spear tip mixture to the top and sprinkle with cheese.
- Bake for 15 minutes until the mushrooms are soft. The mushrooms may sweat a little in the oven, if they do, place them on a paper towel for just a few seconds to absorb the excess moisture, and then place on a serving dish. Serve warm.
- Makes 36 pieces.

Pork Skewers

1 lb. pork tenderloin

1, 8 oz. can pineapple chunks in unsweetened juice

1½ teaspoons curry powder

¼ teaspoon ground cumin

¼ teaspoon paprika

¼ teaspoon cayenne

¼ teaspoon allspice

2 tablespoons olive oil

3 tablespoons lemon juice

1 clove garlic, minced

2 tablespoons fresh minced parsley, to garnish

Nutrition Information Per Serving	
Calories	27.03
Protein	2.56 g.
Carbs	0.62 g.
Fat	1.55 g.

❀ Cut the tenderloin into 1½" cubes and set aside. Drain the pineapple chunks and cut into 1" cubes and set aside.

❀ Combine the spices in a small bowl and mix well. Add the olive oil, garlic and lemon juice to the spice mixture to make a marinade.

❀ Put tenderloin cubes in a mixing bowl, add marinade and stir to coat. Let the pork marinate for 15-30 minutes, stirring occasionally.

❀ Spray a nonstick frying pan with a no stick agent. Turn heat to medium and add pork. Cook, stirring constantly, for 8-10 minutes, until pork is done through.

❀ Remove from heat and thread one piece of pork with one pineapple piece on small party skewers or toothpicks. Garnish with fresh parsley.

❀ Makes 36 pieces.

Spicy Chicken Wings

2 lbs. chicken wings or drumettes

2 tablespoons olive oil

2 teaspoons Lawry's seasoned salt

2 teaspoons citrus & pepper seasoning

1 teaspoon paprika

1 teaspoon cayenne

1 teaspoon ground thyme

Nutrition Information Per Serving	
Calories	233.42
Protein	30.82 g.
Carbs	0.85 g.
Fat	11.08 g.

- ❧ Wash and pat dry chicken wings or drumettes and place in bowl.
- ❧ Pour olive oil over chicken and toss to coat thoroughly.
- ❧ Blend all spices together in small dish and then sprinkle over chicken parts and toss to coat. Use hands to rub spices into chicken skin.
- ❧ Place on a medium grill and grill 6 – 7 minutes a side until desired doneness. These drumettes may also be done in a 375° oven for 20 minutes, turning after about 10 minutes.
- ❧ Makes 8 - 10 servings.

Tip: This recipe of spicy chicken wings is a great, if somewhat messy, appetizer. You may want to serve them with Mustard Dipping Sauce from Chicken Tenders.

Sweet & Spicy Chicken Skewers

1 tablespoon soy sauce

1 tablespoon lemon juice

½ teaspoon allspice

½ teaspoon cinnamon

¼ teaspoon cayenne pepper

⅛ teaspoon paprika

½ teaspoon freshly ground pepper

2 boneless & skinless chicken breasts

½ mango

½ small pineapple

Nutrition Information Per Serving	
Calories	10.16
Protein	1.29 g.
Carbs	1.06 g.
Fat	0.09 g.

- In a shallow bowl combine the soy sauce, lemon juice and spices. Stir to blend well.
- Cut the chicken into 1" square pieces and place in the bowl with sauce. Toss well to coat and let the chicken sit for 10 minutes.
- In a non-stick frying pan, over medium heat, cook the chicken until no longer pink in the middle, approximately 4 – 5 minutes.
- At this point the chicken may be refrigerated for up to 4 hours in an air-tight container.
- Cut the mango and pineapple into 1" pieces and set aside.
- Reheat the chicken by adding a little lemon juice to the bottom of the container and heating gently in the microwave (50% power) for two 45 second bursts and stirring well after each cycle.
- Thread one piece of fruit and one piece of chicken onto individual party toothpicks.
- Makes approximately 48 pieces.

Tangy Shrimp

1, 4½ oz. can of small shrimp

½ cup mayonnaise

2 teaspoons lemon juice

1 teaspoon tomato paste

½ teaspoon Worcestershire Sauce

2 tablespoons fresh minced parsley, divided

1 tablespoon fresh chopped chives

¼ teaspoon paprika

1 English cucumber, sliced

Nutrition Information Per Serving	
Calories	39.07
Protein	1.06 g.
Carbs	0.30 g.
Fat	3.70 g.

- ❀ Whisk together all ingredients for dressing in a small bowl, reserving 1 tablespoon of minced parsley for garnish.
- ❀ Drain shrimp and put into small bowl. Add dressing and mix well. Place small amount of shrimp on cucumber slice and garnish with parsley. You may also use small crackers, although this will add considerably to the carbohydrates.
- ❀ Makes 24 pieces.

SOUPS

Cauliflower, Chive & Garlic Soup

1 medium head cauliflower, about 1½ lbs.

1 medium onion, minced

6 cloves garlic, minced

2 tablespoons olive oil

5 cups chicken or vegetable bouillon

½ cup heavy cream

¼ cup fresh chopped chives

2 tablespoons fresh chopped parsley

1 tablespoon fresh chopped rosemary

1 teaspoon fresh ground pepper

½ teaspoon salt

Nutrition Information Per Serving	
Calories	294.76
Protein	35.38 g.
Carbs	11.63 g.
Fat	8.64 g.

- ❀ Wash cauliflower and cut into florets. Warm olive oil in a large saucepan, and sauté onion, garlic, parsley, salt and pepper and rosemary until onion is soft, about 3 – 4 minutes. Add bouillon and cauliflower and simmer until cauliflower is soft, about 15 minutes.
- ❀ Working in batches, place vegetables and bouillon in food processor and puree. Return to the stove and bring to a boil. Reduce heat and gradually add heavy cream. Add all but a few of the chopped chives and heat thoroughly. Taste and adjust for salt and pepper.
- ❀ Serve with a garnish of fresh chives.
- ❀ Makes 6 servings.

Chicken Soup

4 boneless chicken breasts
6 cups chicken bouillon
2 cups water
4 celery stalks with leaves
1 teaspoon salt
2 teaspoons fresh ground pepper
2 teaspoons butter
½ cup minced onion
1 cup finely chopped celery
2 cups shredded green cabbage
½ cup sliced fresh mushrooms
2 cups fresh chopped vegetables
(broccoli or cauliflower florets, or green
beans, asparagus etc.)
1 medium carrot, thinly sliced

Nutrition Information Per Serving	
Calories	155.23
Protein	22.25 g.
Carbs	7.07 g.
Fat	3.63 g.

- Place 2 cups of bouillon, chicken breasts and celery stalks in a large saucepan over medium high heat. Bring to a boil and reduce heat. Cover and simmer for 20-25 minutes until chicken is cooked through. Remove breasts and set aside. Remove stalks and discard.
- Strain liquid 2 or 3 times until clear. You can strain this liquid through a paper coffee filter to catch the fat. Reserve liquid and set aside.
- Melt butter in the bottom of large saucepan over medium heat. Add onions and mushrooms and sauté for 3-4 minutes.
- Add reserved liquid plus 4 cups of additional chicken bouillon. Add all vegetables, cover and simmer for at least 1 hour. Keep an eye on the pot and add additional liquid in the form of water if the soup appears to be getting too thick.
- Cut the chicken into bite sized pieces and add them to the pot 20 minutes before serving.
- Makes 6 servings.

Cream of Cauliflower Soup

1½ lb. fresh cauliflower

2 tablespoons butter

4 cups chicken bouillon

1 medium sweet onion, minced

1 cup light cream (half & half)

½ cup heavy cream

1 tablespoon fresh chopped thyme

1 tablespoon fresh chopped parsley

1 teaspoon fresh ground pepper

½ teaspoon salt

½ teaspoon paprika

Nutrition Information Per Serving	
Calories	229.81
Protein	5.25 g.
Carbs	5.29 g.
Fat	21.11 g.

To Finish

¼ cup shredded cheddar cheese

1 tablespoon fresh chopped parsley

※ In a large saucepan, over medium heat, sauté onion in butter for 2 – 3 minutes. Add herbs and continue cooking 1 minute longer, stirring constantly. Add chicken broth and cauliflower that has been cut into small pieces. Cover and simmer until cauliflower is soft, about 15 minutes.

※ Process in batches in a food processor until smooth. Return to soup pot and gradually add the creams, paprika and salt and pepper. Heat thoroughly, but do not boil.

※ Garnish with shredded cheese and a sprinkle of fresh chopped parsley.

※ Makes 6 servings.

Tip: This soup may be made 2-3 hours before serving. Refrigerate and reheat before serving. Also good when reheated the next day.

Cream of Mushroom Soup

2 cups fresh mushrooms, cleaned and
finely chopped

3 tablespoons olive oil

1 small red onion, finely chopped

4 cups chicken bouillon

1 tablespoon flour

salt and freshly ground pepper to taste

1 bay leaf

1 teaspoon Fine Herbs

To Finish

1 cup heavy cream

chopped fresh parsley

Nutrition Information Per Serving	
Calories	339.14
Protein	3.35 g.
Carbs	9.12 g.
Fat	33.53 g.

❀ Heat olive oil in heavy saucepan. Cook onions and mushrooms for about 5 minutes, stirring constantly. Add flour and continue cooking for 1 minute.

❀ Gradually add chicken bouillon, stirring constantly. Bring to a boil, lower heat and cover. Gently simmer for 20 minutes.

❀ To Finish: Remove the saucepan from the heat. Remove the bay leave. Adjust salt and pepper to taste. Gradually add the heavy cream and return to medium heat to heat through. Garnish each serving with fresh chopped parsley.

❀ Makes 4 servings.

Creamy Asparagus Soup

2 pounds fresh asparagus
2 cups vegetable bouillon
2 teaspoons olive oil
2 small onions, minced
2 cloves of garlic, minced
1 cup light cream (half & half)
½ cup heavy cream
1 tablespoon lemon zest
To Finish
2 tablespoons sour cream
1 teaspoon heavy cream
freshly ground pepper to taste

Nutrition Information Per Serving	
Calories	327.20
Protein	6.94 g.
Carbs	11.69 g.
Fat	28.59 g.

- ❀ Wash and pat dry asparagus spears. Cut off tough ends and cut 1" tip off each, and reserve. Cut remaining spears into 2" pieces.
- ❀ Bring vegetable bouillon to a boil. Add asparagus spears and cook for approximately 5 minutes. Strain asparagus into a bowl, reserving ¾ cup of broth.
- ❀ Heat oil in a pan over medium heat. Add onion and garlic and sauté for 5 minutes. Add asparagus stalks and cream and simmer 8 minutes until tender.
- ❀ Combine asparagus mixture with reserved broth and process in a blender until smooth. This is a thick and creamy soup.
- ❀ Steam asparagus tips for 2 - 3 minutes until tender.
- ❀ Combine asparagus puree and lemon zest. Simmer over low heat until warmed through.
- ❀ *To Finish:* Serve into individual bowls, add asparagus tips and a swirl of sour cream blended with the heavy cream and freshly ground pepper.
- ❀ Makes 4 servings.

   Tip: The sour cream will lighten up, so that it floats, if blended with a bit of heavy cream before being used.

Creamy Broccoli Soup

1½ lbs. fresh broccoli florets
4 tablespoons butter
4 cups chicken bouillon
1 medium sweet onion, minced
1 cup light cream (half & half)
½ cup heavy cream
1 tablespoon fresh chopped thyme
1 tablespoon fresh chopped chives
1 teaspoon fresh ground pepper
½ teaspoon salt
½ teaspoon ground cumin

Nutrition Information Per Serving	
Calories	186.82
Protein	2.07 g.
Carbs	4.23 g.
Fat	18.52 g.

To Finish
2 tablespoons sour cream
1 teaspoon heavy cream
1 teaspoon fresh chopped parsley

- In a large saucepan, over medium heat, sauté onion in butter for 2 – 3 minutes, until soft. Add herbs and continue cooking 1 minute longer, stirring constantly. Add chicken bouillon and broccoli florets, cut into small pieces. Cover and simmer until broccoli is soft, about 15 minutes.

- Process in batches in a food processor until smooth. Return to soup pot and gradually add the creams, cumin and salt and pepper. Heat thoroughly, but do not boil.

- Garnish with sour cream that has been blended with heavy cream so that it swirls on the soup, and a sprinkle of fresh chopped parsley.

- Makes 8 servings.

  Tip: This soup may be made 2-3 hours before serving. Refrigerate and reheat before serving. Also good when reheated the next day.

Gazpacho Soup

4 cups tomato juice

4 medium tomatoes

2 tablespoons olive oil

2 tablespoons red wine vinegar

1 small red onion, quartered

½ medium sweet green pepper

½ medium cucumber

1 stalk celery, chopped

1 clove garlic, chopped

1 tablespoon each fresh chopped parsley and thyme

1 teaspoon fresh ground pepper

½ teaspoon salt

1 tablespoon sour cream

½ teaspoon heavy cream

fresh chopped parsley to garnish

Nutrition Information Per Serving	
Calories	94.00
Protein	2.20 g.
Carbs	12.07 g.
Fat	5.49 g.

Note: This is a is a wonderful soup on a hot night, and it looks gorgeous with the sour cream and parsley. Thanks to my good friend Kathleen Costello who provided the basic recipe, which I adjusted, just a little.

❖ Peel skin from tomatoes and cut into wedges. Cut cucumber in half lengthwise, remove seeds and cut into 1" pieces.

❖ Working in batches, put half the vegetables and half the tomato juice and other ingredients into a food processor and blend until smooth.

❖ Put batches together in a large bowl and chill. Remove from fridge 5 minutes before serving. If the soup is very thick, you may add some additional tomato juice.

❖ Blend the sour cream with a small amount of heavy cream to lighten consistency. To serve, spoon soup into individual bowls, swirl sour cream mixture on top and add a sprinkle of chopped parsley.

❖ Makes 6 servings.

Summer Squash Soup

3 yellow summer squash (yellow zucchini)

1 tablespoon olive oil

1 large sweet onion, minced

3 cloves of garlic, minced

3 sprigs of lemon thyme (or, 6 sprigs of thyme & 3 strips of lemon peel)

2 cups chicken bouillon

zest & juice of a lemon

¼ teaspoon salt

freshly ground pepper to taste

To Finish

2 tablespoons sour cream

1 teaspoon heavy cream

2 teaspoons lemon zest

4 small sprigs lemon thyme

Nutrition Information Per Serving	
Calories	87.88
Protein	2.75 g.
Carbs	12.27 g.
Fat	4.24 g.

Tip: *The sour cream will lighten up so that it floats, if blended with a bit of heavy cream before being used.*

- ❈ Wash and trim ends of squash. Cut off any blemishes on the skins. Chop coarsely into approximately 1" pieces and set aside.
- ❈ In a large saucepan, heat olive oil over medium heat. Add onions and garlic and sauté for 3 to 4 minutes, or until onions are soft.
- ❈ Add squash and lemon thyme and cook, stirring constantly, for about 5 minutes.
- ❈ Increase heat to medium high. Add chicken bouillon and salt. Cook at a low boil for 20 minutes or until squash is soft.
- ❈ Remove from heat and discard the lemon thyme. Pureé in batches in a blender, and return to saucepan to heat thoroughly. Add the juice of a lemon.
- ❈ *To Finish:* Serve with a garnish of sour cream, a sprinkle of lemon zest, and a sprig of thyme or lemon thyme.
- ❈ Makes 4 servings.

SALADS

Broccoli Salad

3 cups broccoli florets

2 green onions, chopped

1 cup fresh sliced mushrooms

¼ cup roasted pine nuts

½ green pepper, cut into matchsticks

Dressing

½ cup mayonnaise

1 packet Splenda™

3 tablespoons rice wine vinegar

Nutrition Information Per Serving	
Calories	235.12
Protein	2.27 g.
Carbs	6.51 g.
Fat	22.32 g.

- ❀ Steam florets for 2 – 3 minutes until tender crisp, and bright green in color. Plunge into ice water to stop cooking process. Strain and pat dry. Add other ingredients in a large mixing bowl.
- ❀ Whisk together dressing ingredients. Pour over salad and mix well. Chill for at least an hour before serving.
- ❀ Makes 4 servings.

Tip: You may substitute either sweet red pepper or yellow pepper for the green pepper, and this adds a nice note of color.

Chicken Salad

4 boneless, skinless chicken breasts

2 cups chicken bouillon

4 celery stalks with leaves

1 cup finely diced celery

½ cup roasted whole, blanched almonds

½ medium sweet red pepper, cut into match sticks

Nutrition Information Per Serving	
Calories	310.49
Protein	22.49 g.
Carbs	4.04 g.
Fat	22.43 g.

Dressing

½ cup real mayonnaise

4 teaspoons lemon juice

4 – 6 teaspoons reserved poaching liquid

❁ Poach the chicken breasts with the celery stalks in the bouillon for 15 – 20 minutes until completely cooked. Remove from stove top and reserve liquid. The reserved liquid needs to be strained. A paper coffee filter fitted in the strainer works well for straining the fat from the liquid. Put the reserved liquid aside. Place the chicken breasts in the fridge to cool.

❁ Toast the almonds (this can be done in a no-stick frying pan, stirring constantly or in the oven at 350°for 10 – 15 minutes, turning every 5 minutes) and let cool. Chop the celery and red pepper and set aside.

❁ To make the dressing, add the lemon juice and reserved liquid to the mayonnaise until desired consistency is obtained. You may need a little more reserved liquid, depending upon desired thickness of dressing.

continued next page

Chicken Salad cont.

❀ Remove the chicken from fridge and cut into bite sized pieces. Put chicken, almonds, celery and red pepper in a large bowl and mix with dressing until well coated. This salad will keep in a covered bowl in the fridge for up to 2 days.

❀ Makes 6 servings.

Note: This recipe comes from my good friend Pearl Rudin in Toronto. Pearl says that originally it came from an old New York Times Cookbook and that she adjusted it slightly. I made some further minor revisions to Pearl's version.

Tip: A nice variation is to replace the reserved liquid with raspberry vinegar in the dressing. This provides some tang and a bit of color to the dressing.

Chicken with Pineapple

2 cups cooked white chicken meat, cut up

2 green onions, chopped

2 celery stalks, finely minced

½ cup unsalted cashews, coarsely chopped

¼ cup pineapple chunks, chopped

Dressing

½ cup mayonnaise

1 tablespoon lemon juice

1 tablespoon unsweetened pineapple juice

½ teaspoon curry powder

1 tablespoon fresh chopped parsley

Nutrition Information Per Serving	
Calories	385.16
Protein	17.38 g.
Carbs	9.63 g.
Fat	30.77 g.

❀ Cut the chicken into bite-sized pieces and mix together with other ingredients in a bowl. (I use canned pineapple chunks in unsweetened pineapple juice. I drain the chunks, reserving the liquid for use in the dressing, and cut the chunks into smaller pieces.)

❀ Whisk together all ingredients for the dressing. Combine with the chicken and mix well.

❀ Serve on a bed of red leaf lettuce, with a couple of cherry tomatoes for color.

❀ Makes 4 servings.

Tip: 2 large boneless, skinless breasts that have been poached work well for this salad.

Crab Salad

8 oz. crab meat

2 medium tomatoes

1 medium red onion, thinly sliced

16 fresh asparagus spears

6 cups green leaf lettuce

Dijon Vinaigrette

Dijon Vinaigrette

⅓ cup olive oil

4 tablespoons white wine vinegar

2 tablespoons lemon juice

1 teaspoon Dijon mustard

1 teaspoon each, fresh chopped rosemary & thyme

2 teaspoons fresh chopped parsley

1 packet Splenda™

Nutrition Information Per Serving	
Calories	267.82
Protein	15.16 g.
Carbs	9.55 g.
Fat	20.08 g.

- Wash asparagus and cut tough ends off. Place in boiling water for 2 – 3 minutes until tender crisp. Drain and plunge into ice water until cool. Wrap in paper towel and set aside.
- Whisk together all ingredients for dressing.
- Divide the lettuce evenly and arrange in an attractive layer on each plate. Layer the ingredients as follows: tomato, separated onion rings, and 4 asparagus spears across the top of each salad. At this point drizzle the salad with the Dijon Vinaigrette. Sprinkle the crab meat across the top of the asparagus.
- Makes 4 servings.

Cucumber Salad

1 small English cucumber

1 small green or sweet red pepper

Dressing

¼ cup white wine vinegar

1 tablespoon olive oil

1 teaspoon dry mustard

1 teaspoon fresh chopped parsley

Nutrition Information Per Serving	
Calories	55.16
Protein	0.81 g.
Carbs	4.90 g.
Fat	3.66 g.

❊ Thinly slice the cucumber. Cut green pepper into matchstick pieces.

❊ Whisk together dressing ingredients and toss with vegetables. Serve chilled.

❊ Makes 4 servings.

Curried Chicken Salad

2 cups cooked white chicken meat, cut up

2 green onions, chopped

2 celery stalks, finely minced

⅓ cup unsalted cashews, coarsely chopped

¼ cup seedless raisins

Dressing

½ cup real mayonnaise

2 tablespoons lemon juice

½ teaspoon curry powder

1 tablespoon fresh chopped parsley

Nutrition Information Per Serving	
Calories	369.80
Protein	32.81 g.
Carbs	11.24 g.
Fat	20.99 g.

* Cut the chicken into bite-sized pieces and mix together with other ingredients in a bowl.
* Whisk together all ingredients for the dressing. Combine with the chicken and mix well.
* Serve on a bed of leaf lettuce, with some sliced cucumber for contrast.
* Makes 4 servings.

Tip: 2 large boneless, skinless breasts that have been poached work well for this salad.

Note: The raisins really add to the carbohydrate count. They can be reduced, and the carbohydrate count will fall.

Easy Coleslaw

4 cups finely sliced green cabbage

2 cups finely sliced red cabbage

Nutrition Information Per Serving	
Calories	95.27
Protein	0.81 g.
Carbs	3.47 g.
Fat	8.95 g.

Easy Coleslaw Dressing

½ cup real mayonnaise

1½ tablespoons lemon juice

1 tablespoon lime juice

❀ Whisk together dressing ingredients in a small bowl. Combine dressing with cabbage in a large bowl and mix well.

❀ Chill for at least an hour before serving to allow flavors to blend. Will keep up to 48 hours in a fridge.

❀ Makes 8 – 10 servings.

Tip: To keep the red color from running, rinse the sliced red cabbage under cold water in a colander, until the water runs clear.

Fancy Coleslaw

6 cups finely sliced green cabbage

1 cup finely sliced red cabbage

1 medium carrot, finely shredded

½ medium sweet red pepper, cut into matchsticks

Fancy Coleslaw Dressing

½ cup real mayonnaise

1 tablespoon lemon juice

1 tablespoon white wine vinegar

1 packet Splenda™

Nutrition Information Per Serving	
Calories	99.02
Protein	0.88 g.
Carbs	4.36 g.
Fat	8.97 g.

- ❂ Whisk together dressing ingredients.
- ❂ Wash and prepare vegetables and put in a large bowl. Add dressing to vegetables and combine well.
- ❂ Chill for at least an hour before serving to allow flavors to blend. Will keep up to 48 hours in a fridge.
- ❂ Makes 8 – 10 servings.

Tip: To keep the red color from running, rinse the sliced red cabbage under cold water in a colander, until the water runs clear.

Green Bean and Almond Salad

3 cups green beans (about 1 lb.)

½ cup roasted almond pieces

1 medium sweet red pepper, cut into matchsticks

White Wine Vinaigrette

⅓ cup olive oil

⅓ cup white wine vinegar

1 teaspoon Dijon mustard

1 teaspoon fresh ground pepper

1 packet Splenda™

Nutrition Information Per Serving	
Calories	189.80
Protein	3.14 g.
Carbs	7.91 g.
Fat	17.41 g.

❀ Wash and trim beans. Cut into 2-3" pieces. Plunge beans into boiling water and leave for 3-4 minutes until bright green and crispy tender. Drain and immediately put into large bowl of ice water. Strain and pat dry.

❀ Put beans, almond pieces and red pepper into a large bowl.

❀ Whisk together dressing ingredients and pour over vegetables. Stir well to blend flavors. Serve chilled.

❀ Makes 6 servings.

Greens With Pecans & Blue Cheese

6 cups washed, mixed wild greens

½ cup roasted pecan halves

4 oz. blue cheese

Raspberry Vinaigrette

1 teaspoon dry mustard

2 teaspoons fresh chopped parsley

¼ teaspoon salt

4 tablespoons olive oil

4 tablespoons raspberry vinegar

Nutrition Information Per Serving	
Calories	328.0
Protein	8.05 g.
Carbs	5.97 g.
Fat	31.53 g.

❋ Combine all vinaigrette ingredients in a jar or salad dressing container and shake vigorously for 30 seconds or until well blended. This recipe makes sufficient dressing for 4 salads.

❋ Clean and trim greens and place in large salad bowl. Toss greens with raspberry vinaigrette dressing.

❋ Arrange greens on 4 individual salad plates. Sprinkle with pecan halves, evenly divided among the servings. Crumble blue cheese on top of the greens.

❋ Makes 4 servings.

Grilled Asparagus Salad

6 cups wild greens

16 asparagus spears

1 small sweet red pepper

½ small sweet yellow pepper

2 tablespoons olive oil

½ teaspoon fresh ground pepper

¼ cup toasted pecans, chopped

Balsamic Vinaigrette

¼ cup olive oil

⅓ cup balsamic vinegar

1 teaspoon dry mustard

1 teaspoon fresh chopped parsley

1 packet Splenda™

½ teaspoon fresh ground pepper

Nutrition Information Per Serving	
Calories	180.23
Protein	4.16 g.
Carbs	11.76 g.
Fat	14.52 g.

❀ Preheat grill to medium heat. Cut peppers into quarters and remove all seeds and extra pulp. Brush asparagus and peppers with olive oil and sprinkle asparagus with some fresh ground pepper. Grill over medium heat for 3 – 4 minutes a side, watching carefully. You want the vegetables to be soft and have grill marks without being overdone. Set aside to cool.

❀ Clean greens and slice grilled peppers. Mix together in a large bowl.

❀ Whisk together the vinaigrette and toss with greens, reserving a small amount of dressing.

❀ Divide salad evenly among 4 plates. Arrange the asparagus spears attractively on top of the greens, sprinkle with toasted pecans and drizzle with the remaining dressing.

❀ Makes 4 servings.

Grilled Chicken Salad

4 boneless, skinless chicken breasts

½ cup marinade (orange, lemon or other.)

6 cups mixed fresh greens

2 hard boiled eggs

4 celery stalks, chopped

4 oz. cheese cut into bite sized pieces
(brie or similar type)

½ medium sweet red pepper, thinly sliced

½ cucumber, thinly sliced

¼ cup toasted almond slices

½ cup Raspberry Vinaigrette
(See Table of Contents)
or other dressing of choice

Nutrition Information Per Serving	
Calories	455.86
Protein	44.51 g.
Carbs	10.66 g.
Fat	26.62 g.

❀ Marinate chicken breasts in shallow bowl for at least 30 minutes.

❀ Preheat grill to medium high. (Breasts may also be done in a medium hot frying pan with 1 tablespoon of olive oil.)

❀ Clean greens and distribute evenly among 4 plates. Cut eggs into slices and arrange around the perimeter of the plate.

❀ Divide and arrange the cheese and other vegetables attractively on top of the greens.

❀ Grill (or fry) the chicken breasts for 4 – 5 minutes each side until cooked through. Remove from heat and slice into thin slices, on the diagonal.

❀ Pour dressing over greens and place sliced hot chicken on top of greens. Sprinkle with toasted almond slivers.

❀ Makes 4 servings.

Salmon Salad

2 cups cooked, cut-up salmon

2 green onions, finely chopped

2 celery stalks, finely diced

Dressing

½ cup mayonnaise

3 teaspoons fresh lemon juice

2 packets Splenda™

1 tablespoon fresh chopped dill

½ teaspoon fresh ground pepper

Nutrition Information Per Serving	
Calories	352.13
Protein	22.46 g.
Carbs	2.61 g.
Fat	29.25 g.

❀ Cut salmon into bite sized pieces and put into a bowl with onion and celery.

❀ Whisk together all dressing ingredients in a small bowl. Pour dressing over salmon and mix well.

❀ Serve over a bed of butter lettuce.

❀ Makes 4 servings.

Savory Coleslaw

4 cups finely sliced green cabbage

2 cups finely sliced red cabbage

2 green onions, thinly sliced

Savory Coleslaw Dressing

½ cup real mayonnaise

1 tablespoon lemon juice

1 clove of garlic, minced

1 tablespoon white wine vinegar

Nutrition Information Per Serving	
Calories	96.30
Protein	0.85 g.
Carbs	3.55 g.
Fat	8.97 g.

❁ Whisk together dressing ingredients until smooth and set aside.

❁ Cut cabbage and onion into very thin slices and mix in a large bowl with dressing.

❁ Chill for at least an hour before serving to allow flavors to blend. Will keep up to 48 hours in a fridge.

❁ Makes 8 – 10 servings.

Tip: To keep the red color from running, rinse the sliced red cabbage under cold water in a colander, until the water runs clear.

Spinach Salad

6 cups fresh spinach

2 hard boiled eggs

4 slices of bacon

1 cup sliced raw mushrooms

½ cup roasted almond pieces

1 small sweet red pepper, cut into matchsticks

Spinach Salad Dressing

¹/₃ cup olive oil

2 tablespoons red wine vinegar

1 clove garlic, finely minced

1 teaspoon dry mustard

1 packet Splenda™

½ teaspoon salt

½ teaspoon fresh ground pepper

Nutrition Information Per Serving	
Calories	348.40
Protein	10.73 g.
Carbs	8.08 g.
Fat	31.69 g.

❀ Wash and pat dry the spinach. Cook bacon until crispy and let cool, then chop into pieces. Chop the eggs into small pieces. Combine all ingredients in a large bowl.

❀ Whisk together all ingredients for the dressing to emulsify. Add the dressing to the salad just before serving.

❀ Makes 4 servings.

Note: The recipe for the dressing came from Robin Hartzell, who adapted it from her favorite.

Summer Salad

5 cups mixed wild greens

1 cup red leaf lettuce

½ medium pear, quartered and thinly sliced

½ cup palm hearts (canned)

1 small avocado, peeled and thinly sliced

To Finish

3 tablespoons fresh chopped flat parsley

Balsamic & Raspberry Vinaigrette

1½ tablespoons balsamic vinegar

1½ tablespoons raspberry vinegar

1½ tablespoons lemon juice

½ tablespoon fresh chopped flat parsley

$^1/_3$ cup olive oil

Nutrition Information Per Serving	
Calories	273.42
Protein	2.54 g.
Carbs	10.30 g.
Fat	26.55 g.

❀ Prepare all vegetables in a large salad bowl.

❀ Whisk together ingredients for dressing until blended and pour over salad. Toss to coat with dressing and sprinkle with fresh parsley. Divide evenly among serving plates.

❀ Makes 4 servings.

Tip: To make a quick vinaigrette dressing, place all ingredients in a small glass jar. Put the lid on tightly and shake vigorously for 30 seconds to mix.

Tangy Coleslaw

2 cups finely chopped green cabbage

1 cup finely chopped red cabbage

1 medium carrot, grated

2 green onions, thinly sliced

Tangy Coleslaw Dressing

½ cup olive oil

⅓ cup white wine vinegar

1½ teaspoons dry mustard

1 teaspoon ground pepper

1 tablespoon fresh chopped parsley

1 clove garlic, finely minced

Nutrition Information Per Serving	
Calories	138.92
Protein	0.49 g.
Carbs	2.96 g.
Fat	14.13 g.

❈ Place the cabbage in a large mixing bowl and add grated carrot and green onion. (I prefer the cabbage to be finely chopped, but you may shred it if you prefer your slaw in very fine pieces.)

❈ Whisk together all ingredients for the dressing. Pour over cabbage and mix well. Let stand in the fridge for at least an hour, before serving.

❈ This tastes better the second day, when all the flavors have blended.

❈ Makes 6 – 8 servings.

Tip: To keep the red color from running, rinse the sliced red cabbage under cold water in a colander, until the water runs clear.

Tuna Salad

2, 6 oz. cans of tuna

¼ cup mayonnaise

2 tablespoons lemon juice

1 packet Splenda™

1 tablespoon fresh chopped parsley

1 celery stalk, diced

½ cup finely chopped green onion

6 cups red leaf lettuce

2 ripe tomatoes

Nutrition Information Per Serving	
Calories	278.67
Protein	25.16 g.
Carbs	2.44 g.
Fat	19.13 g.

- Whisk together the mayonnaise, Splenda™, lemon juice and parsley and set aside. Mix together tuna, onion and celery in a mixing bowl. Fold together the dressing with the tuna mixture.
- Evenly distribute the tuna salad over a bed of lettuce. Garnish with tomato wedges.
- Makes 4 servings.

Waldorf Salad

2 cups cooked, cut-up chicken

2 celery stalks, cut on an angle

½ cup walnut pieces

1 small ripe avocado

6 cups fresh greens

Waldorf Dressing

⅓ cup mayonnaise

2 tablespoons heavy cream

1 tablespoon white wine vinegar

1 packet Splenda™

½ teaspoon salt

½ teaspoon freshly ground pepper

Nutrition Information Per Serving	
Calories	414.85
Protein	18.15 g.
Carbs	11.59 g.
Fat	34.24 g.

- ❈ Whisk together all ingredients for the dressing and set aside.
- ❈ Skin and pit the avocado and cut into thin slices. Combine the cut-up chicken, walnuts, celery and avocado in a large mixing bowl. Mix with the dressing.
- ❈ Serve on a bed of fresh greens.
- ❈ Makes 4 servings.

Note: This is a delicious alternative to the regular Waldorf with its high carb apple slivers. To reduce the calories, use only half an avocado in the salad.

VEGETABLES

Asparagus with Balsamic Vinegar

1 lb. asparagus

1 tablespoon olive oil

2 garlic cloves, minced

2 tablespoons butter

4 tablespoons balsamic vinegar

4 tablespoons water

1 tablespoon fresh chopped parsley

1 teaspoon fresh ground pepper

Nutrition Information Per Serving	
Calories	113.67
Protein	2.70 g.
Carbs	5.87 g.
Fat	9.50 g.

❈ Heat oil in a nonstick frying pan over medium heat. Add garlic and parsley and cook for 2 minutes, stirring constantly. Add balsamic vinegar, water and butter to the pan and cook until blended, about 1 minute.

❈ Add the asparagus and pepper to the pan and simmer until tender, approximately 5 minutes.

❈ Place asparagus on plates.

❈ Makes 4 servings.

Broccoli Soufflé

4 eggs, separated

1 cup broccoli florets

½ cup shredded cheddar cheese

1 cup light cream (half & half)

1 tablespoon flour

½ teaspoon salt

1 tablespoon sour cream

1 teaspoon heavy cream

Nutrition Information Per Serving	
Calories	237.55
Protein	13.32 g.
Carbs	6.66 g.
Fat	17.82 g.

※ Preheat oven to 300°. Steam florets for 10 minutes or until soft. Put florets in a food processor with sour cream and heavy cream and puree. Set aside. You will have about ½ cup of the puree.

※ In the top of a double boiler, over boiling water, heat light cream for 2 – 3 minutes. Whisk in flour until smooth and thickened, about 3 minutes. Add shredded cheese and whisk until completely blended, about 5 minutes. Remove from heat.

※ In a large separate bowl, beat egg whites until very stiff. Add egg yolks to the cheese mixture, one at a time, whisking after each addition. Fold in the pureed broccoli to the cheese mixture.

※ Gradually, working in 4 – 5 batches, fold the cheese and broccoli mixture into the egg white.

※ Pour into an ungreased, 1½ quart casserole dish, until ¼" from the top.

※ Place casserole in the center of the oven and bake for 60 minutes. Do not open oven door while soufflé is baking. Serve at once.

※ Makes 4 servings.

Note: This makes a lovely lunch with a small green salad. It is also a nice vegetable as an accompaniment to a chicken dish.

Variation: For a two cheese soufflé, cut out the broccoli puree and substitute a ½ cup of another shredded cheese, like a Swiss cheese.

Broccoli Supreme

¾ lb. broccoli florets

2 cups chicken bouillon

1 tablespoon butter

½ medium, sweet onion, diced

1 tablespoon fresh chopped parsley

½ tablespoon each fresh chopped chives, thyme

⅓ cup sour cream

¼ cup heavy cream

1 teaspoon fresh ground pepper

salt to taste

fresh chopped parsley to garnish

Nutrition Information Per Serving	
Calories	124.21
Protein	0.71 g.
Carbs	3.37 g.
Fat	12.44 g.

- ❀ Bring the chicken bouillon to a boil and add the florets. Cover and simmer until the florets are soft, about 15 minutes.
- ❀ While the broccoli is simmering, in a small saucepan, melt butter over medium heat. Sauté onions until soft, about 4 minutes. Add fresh herbs and sauté for a minute longer. Remove from heat and set aside.
- ❀ Drain the broccoli and place it in a food processor with the onion and herb mixture, as well as the sour cream and heavy cream. Process until smooth.
- ❀ The broccoli may be refrigerated at this point, or frozen when cooled and then reheated when ready to serve.
- ❀ If serving right away, return to the stove over a low heat to keep warm. Garnish with fresh chopped parsley.
- ❀ Makes 4 servings.

Note: This is a very tasty side dish that is a rich dark green in color and looks wonderful on a plate. Special thanks to my friend Pearl Rudin for the idea for this dish.

Creamy Garlic Cauliflower

1 medium head of cauliflower
(about 4 cups of florets)

1 medium onion, minced

2 cups chicken bouillon

2 garlic cloves, minced

2 teaspoons butter

¼ cup sour cream

¼ cup heavy cream

1 tablespoon fresh chopped chives or parsley

Nutrition Information Per Serving (6 servings)	
Calories	83.06
Protein	1.22 g.
Carbs	3.51 g.
Fat	7.12 g.

❊ Wash cauliflower and cut into small florets. Bring chicken bouillon to a boil in a large saucepan and add cauliflower. Simmer until soft, about 15 minutes.

❊ While cauliflower is simmering, sauté onion and garlic in 1 teaspoon of butter in a small saucepan over medium heat. Cook until soft, about 3 – 4 minutes.

❊ Drain cauliflower when soft. Add cauliflower, onion and garlic, as well as sour cream, heavy cream and additional teaspoon of butter to a food processor and process until smooth. You may have to process in batches, depending on the size of your processor.

❊ At this point the cauliflower may be refrigerated or frozen until ready to use. If using immediately, reheat gently in original saucepan. Serve sprinkled with chopped chives or parsley.

❊ Makes 4 – 6 servings.

Tip: This is a great substitute for mashed potatoes, and I often serve it with meatloaf, for just this reason.

Garlic Cauliflower with Pine Nuts

1½ – 2 lbs. cauliflower

2 teaspoons fresh lemon juice

⅓ cup olive oil

1 teaspoon paprika

2 cups water

1 teaspoon salt

1 teaspoon freshly ground pepper

2 garlic cloves, minced

½ cup pine nuts, coarsely chopped

2 tablespoons fresh chopped parsley

Nutrition Information Per Serving	
Calories	181.74
Protein	4.49 g.
Carbs	9.48 g.
Fat	15.68 g.

※ An hour before serving, fill a large bowl with water and add the lemon juice. Wash the cauliflower and cut into florets. Place cauliflower in the liquid and set aside.

※ 20 minutes before serving, heat the olive oil in a large nonstick frying pan over medium heat. Add the paprika and garlic and cook for 1 – 2 minutes. Add the 2 cups of water and bring to a boil. Drain the cauliflower from the cold water and add to the boiling water in the pan. Season with salt and cook uncovered until cauliflower is tender, approximately 15 minutes.

※ Add the chopped nuts and the fresh parsley. Season with salt and pepper and continue cooking for 2 minutes longer. The liquid evaporates while cooking. Serve on individual plates.

※ Makes 6 servings.

Green Beans with Bacon & Mushrooms

1 lb. fresh green beans

1 teaspoon olive oil

½ cup finely diced fresh mushrooms

4 slices of bacon chopped into ¼" slices

2 green onions cut into ¼" pieces

fresh ground pepper to taste

To Finish

¼ cup heavy cream

fresh chopped parsley to garnish

Nutrition Information Per Serving	
Calories	91.14
Protein	4.87 g.
Carbs	9.31 g.
Fat	4.42 g.

- ❋ Clean and trim beans to desired size. Steam beans until just tender, about 4 – 6 minutes. Pat dry on a paper towel and put to one side.
- ❋ Heat olive oil in a large fry pan or saucepan, over medium heat. Sauté bacon, mushrooms and onion until cooked, about 3 – 5 minutes. Stir in beans and season with pepper. Add cream and heat through while stirring constantly, about 2 – 3 minutes.
- ❋ Transfer to serving platter or individual plates and garnish with chopped parsley.
- ❋ Makes 4 servings.

Green Beans in Curry

1 lb. fresh green beans

1,14 oz. can of coconut milk

¼ cup minced onion

1 clove garlic, finely minced

1 teaspoon curry powder

½ teaspoon cumin

½ teaspoon olive oil

Nutrition Information Per Serving	
Calories	162.02
Protein	2.90 g.
Carbs	8.27 g.
Fat	14.69 g.

❀ Heat oil in heavy frying pan, over medium high heat. Sauté garlic and onion for 2 – 3 minutes until soft. Although this is a small amount of oil, the onions will sweat and release moisture as they cook. Add coconut milk and spices and bring mixture to a boil.

❀ Add trimmed green beans to the milk, cover and simmer for 10 minutes.

❀ Makes 6 servings.

Green Beans with Mustard

¾ lb. green beans

2 teaspoons olive oil

1½ teaspoons Dijon mustard

2 garlic cloves, finely minced

Nutrition Information Per Serving	
Calories	25.00
Protein	0.54 g.
Carbs	1.13 g.
Fat	2.72 g.

❀ Clean and trim beans. Add beans to a pot of boiling water and cook for just 2 – 3 minutes until tender crisp. Drain beans and set aside in a container.

❀ Heat oil in a large nonstick frying pan over medium heat. Add garlic and mustard and stir for 1 minute. Add beans and continue cooking, while stirring, for another 4 – 5 minutes.

❀ Makes 4 servings.

Green Beans with Onions & Vinegar

1 lb. green beans

1 medium red onion, thinly sliced

1 teaspoon fresh ground pepper

2 tablespoons olive oil

3 tablespoons red wine vinegar

1 teaspoon Dijon mustard

Nutrition Information Per Serving	
Calories	38.40
Protein	0.70 g.
Carbs	3.58 g.
Fat	2.64 g.

❀ Clean and trim green beans. Bring 2 cups of water to boil in a large saucepan. Add beans and cook until just tender-crisp, about 3 – 4 minutes. Drain and set aside briefly.

❀ In a large frying pan, heat oil over medium high heat. Sauté onion for 3 – 4 minutes and then add beans. Whisk together mustard and red wine vinegar. Add to the pan and stir well while continuing to cook for 2 minutes longer.

❀ Makes 4 servings.

Grilled Asparagus with Lemon Butter

1 lb. fresh asparagus
2 tablespoons butter
1 teaspoon fresh lemon juice
1 teaspoon fresh chopped parsley
2 tablespoons olive oil
3 teaspoons fresh lemon juice
1 tablespoon fresh chopped mint
1 garlic clove, finely minced

Nutrition Information Per Serving	
Calories	138.50
Protein	2.72 g.
Carbs	5.48 g.
Fat	13.00 g.

※ At least an hour before serving, bring butter to room temperature. Add the lemon juice and fresh parsley and mix well. Swirl into small rounds and place on waxed paper. Place in the fridge to harden.

※ Wash and trim the ends of the asparagus. Using wooden skewers that have been soaked in water for at least an hour, thread two parallel skewers through 4 asparagus. Alternately, use a grilling basket or rack to grill the asparagus.

※ Whisk together the olive oil, mint, garlic and lemon juice.

※ Place the skewered asparagus on a shallow serving plate and pour over the olive oil mixture. Turn to coat and let sit for 30 minutes at room temperature.

※ Preheat BBQ to medium. Brush the asparagus with any remaining marinade and place on the grill. Brush remaining liquid on the upside. Turn asparagus after 2 – 3 minutes and grill for an additional 2 – 3 minutes. Do not leave the grill as these delicious vegetables can burn very easily.

※ Remove from grill and slide off the skewers. Place on plates and put a patty of lemon butter on each bunch of asparagus.

※ Makes 4 servings.

Tip: For grilling, you will want to choose large asparagus, unlike when you are steaming them and looking for the small tender ones. The asparagus can be grilled without being skewered, this just makes them easier to handle. The lemon butter can be used on many different vegetables, and fish.

Grilled Zucchini

2 medium zucchini

2 tablespoons olive oil

¼ teaspoon paprika

½ teaspoon dried parsley

½ teaspoon dried thyme

1 teaspoon fresh ground pepper

Nutrition Information Per Serving	
Calories	81.94
Protein	1.23 g.
Carbs	3.42 g.
Fat	7.22 g.

❀ Preheat grill to medium high. Add spices to olive oil in small dish.

❀ Cut zucchini in half, lengthwise. Brush both sides of zucchini with olive oil mixture.

❀ Place zucchini on grill, cut side down. Grill for 2 – 3 minutes a side, depending upon thickness. Test with fork to determine doneness.

❀ Makes 4 servings.

Lemon Cabbage

2 tablespoons olive oil

1 medium head of green cabbage

juice of one lemon + 1 tablespoon lemon zest

1 cup fresh snow peas, washed and trimmed

1 cup chicken bouillon

salt & freshly ground pepper to taste

Nutrition Information Per Serving	
Calories	109.0
Protein	4.37 g.
Carbs	7.13 g.
Fat	11.4 g.

- ❈ Wash cabbage and slice thinly into bite sized pieces.
- ❈ Heat olive oil in large frying pan. Add cabbage and sprinkle with lemon juice and zest. Add salt and pepper to taste.
- ❈ Cook, stirring constantly, for 2 – 3 minutes. Mix in trimmed snow peas. Simmer gently, stirring occasionally, for 5 – 6 minutes until cabbage is tender.
- ❈ Serve using slotted spoon to drain.
- ❈ Cabbage should be tender but crisp.
- ❈ Makes 4 servings.

Tip: The snow peas add color and carbohydrates. To reduce the carbohydrates, leave out the snow peas.

Mushroom & Cheese Omelet

2 eggs

2 teaspoons butter

1 tablespoon water

½ cup sliced fresh mushrooms

¼ cup shredded cheddar cheese

fresh ground pepper and salt to taste

Nutrition Information Per Serving	
Calories	350.35
Protein	21.85 g.
Carbs	4.00 g.
Fat	27.19 g.

❋ Melt 1 teaspoon of butter in small frying pan and sauté mushrooms until soft. Set aside, but keep warm.

❋ Add water to eggs and beat with whisk until smooth. Add ground pepper and salt to taste.

❋ Wipe out frying pan and add second teaspoon of butter and melt over medium heat. Rotate pan to ensure that butter coats bottom and sides evenly.

❋ Pour eggs into pan, rotating to ensure that the bottom is evenly distributed. As egg sets around the edges, lift with a spatula to allow uncooked egg to run under edges. When egg is mostly cooked, add mushrooms and cheese. Slip spatula under one side and gently fold omelet over to form half moon and let sit for another minute to melt cheese. Using spatula, slide omelet onto serving dish.

❋ Makes 1 serving.

Variations: The following fillings can be used to vary the omelet.
Peppers: Sautéed chopped red and green peppers.
Fine Herbs: Freshly chopped parsley, chives and thyme.
Western: Ham, green pepper and onion.
Vegetable: Sautéed green onion, zucchini and cheese,
or any vegetable you like.

Note: This omelet can be made with egg beaters, or just egg whites if preferred.

Mushroom & Spinach Frittata

1 teaspoon butter

1 small onion, halved & sliced

1 cup fresh sliced mushrooms

1 cup cooked fresh spinach, chopped

1 tablespoon fresh chopped parsley

⅛ teaspoon cayenne

8 eggs, beaten

¼ cup light cream (half & half)

½ teaspoon Dijon mustard

½ teaspoon salt

1 teaspoon fresh ground pepper

½ cup shredded cheddar cheese

1 tablespoon toasted pine nuts

Nutrition Information Per Serving	
Calories	179.75
Protein	12.71 g.
Carbs	3.66 g.
Fat	12.42 g.

※ Preheat oven to 375°. Lightly grease a 9" glass pie plate. Melt butter in a non-stick frying pan over medium heat. Add onion and mushrooms and sauté until soft, approximately 5 minutes. Remove from heat and add the cooked chopped spinach, parsley and cayenne.

※ In a bowl, whisk the eggs, half & half, mustard, salt and pepper. Stir in the vegetable mixture and cheese. Pour mixture into the pie plate and sprinkle with pine nuts.

※ Bake for 25 to 30 minutes until top is nicely browned. Remove from oven and serve immediately.

※ Makes 6 servings.

Note: This is a gorgeous looking, browned egg and vegetable dish, reminiscent of a quiche without the pastry. It can be served either for breakfast or lunch.

Red Cabbage Casserole

1 small turnip (about 1 lb.)

1 head red cabbage (about 1½ lbs.)

1 medium sweet onion, sliced thinly

¼ cup toasted almond slivers

1 packet Splenda™

1½ cups chicken bouillon

½ cup white wine

salt & fresh ground pepper to taste

Nutrition Information Per Serving	
Calories	68.88
Protein	2.75 g.
Carbs	9.84 g.
Fat	2.39 g.

❀ Preheat oven to 350°.

❀ Wash, trim and thinly slice the cabbage. Julienne the turnip and place all vegetables and the almond pieces in an oven proof casserole. Add salt and pepper.

❀ Mix the bouillon, wine and Splenda™. Pour over vegetables in the casserole and mix well.

❀ Bake for one hour, or until the cabbage is tender.

❀ Makes 8 servings.

Tip: This recipe can be reheated in the oven or microwave on the following day, if there are leftovers.

Spicy Oven Baked Zucchini

1 medium zucchini (10 – 12" long)

2 tablespoons olive oil

2 tablespoons Mrs. Dash Extra Spicy

Nutrition Information Per Serving	
Calories	148.22
Protein	1.29 g.
Carbs	3.39 g.
Fat	14.29 g.

※ Preheat oven to 350°

※ Clean and pat dry zucchini. Cut in half lengthways, and cut into ½" pieces.

※ Place zucchini pieces in deep bowl and pour olive oil into bowl. Stir to coat with the oil. Add Mrs. Dash Extra Spicy, and stir well to coat zucchini.

※ Place zucchini on a cookie sheet sprayed with a no-stick agent.

※ Bake for 12 – 15 minutes, or until zucchini is soft when a fork is inserted. The zucchini will be brown on the underside.

※ Makes 2 servings.

Note: Thanks to my daughter-in-law, Sian Haakonson, who was the inspiration for this vegetable dish.

Vegetables in Balsamic Vinegar

8 large mushrooms, stems removed

8, ½" slices of eggplant

1 red onion, cut into quarters

8 asparagus spears

½ cup olive oil

4 tablespoons balsamic vinegar

1 teaspoon dry mustard

2 teaspoons fresh chopped thyme

Nutrition Information Per Serving	
Calories	301.93
Protein	3.07 g.
Carbs	11.93 g.
Fat	28.64 g.

❀ Preheat oven to 350°.

❀ Combine olive oil, vinegar, mustard and thyme. Place vegetables in a shallow bowl, and pour marinade over them, turning to coat.

❀ Place vegetables in a roasting pan that has been sprayed with a no-stick agent. Brush any marinade that remains in the shallow bowl over the vegetables.

❀ Bake for 35 – 40 minutes or until all vegetables are cooked, turning once after 20 minutes or so.

❀ Makes 4 servings.

Vegetable Medley

1 cup yellow zucchini pieces

1 cup green zucchini pieces

1 medium red onion, sliced

½ red pepper, thinly sliced

1 cup of green beans or asparagus spears

1 tablespoon olive oil

salt & freshly ground pepper to taste

Nutrition Information Per Serving	
Calories	66.86
Protein	1.68 g.
Carbs	8.27 g.
Fat	3.79 g.

❀ Clean and trim all vegetables.

❀ Heat olive oil over medium heat in a heavy frying pan.

❀ Add vegetables with salt and pepper and sauté for 4 – 6 minutes, until tender.

❀ Makes 4 servings.

Zucchini with Tomatoes

3 medium zucchini (about 1½ lbs.)

2 tablespoons olive oil

1 medium red onion, quartered and then thinly sliced

½ cup white wine

2 medium tomatoes, coarsely chopped

1 tablespoon each, fresh chopped parsley & thyme

1 clove garlic, minced

½ teaspoon fresh ground pepper

1 packet Splenda™

Nutrition Information Per Serving	
Calories	109.86
Protein	2.79 g.
Carbs	9.41 g.
Fat	7.42 g.

❀ In a small bowl, combine tomatoes, garlic, parsley, thyme and pepper. Sprinkle with Splenda™ and toss to coat. Let stand for 15 minutes.

❀ Cut zucchini in half lengthwise, and then into ½" slices. In a large frying pan, heat oil over medium high heat. Cook zucchini and onion in oil for 2 – 3 minutes, until just beginning to brown. Add the wine, reduce heat and simmer for 5 minutes until the zucchini is soft and the wine is reduced by half.

❀ Add the tomato mixture to the zucchini and cook until heated through, about 2 minutes.

❀ Makes 4 servings.

POULTRY

Chicken Breasts with Peppers and Mushrooms

4 boneless, skinless chicken breasts
1 green pepper, thinly sliced
1 medium sweet onion, thinly sliced
2 cups fresh mushrooms, sliced
1 tablespoon olive oil
½ cup chicken bouillon
1 tablespoon butter
¼ cup white wine or sherry
¼ cup heavy cream
1 tablespoon each fresh chopped
rosemary & thyme
1 teaspoon fresh ground pepper

Nutrition Information Per Serving	
Calories	294.35
Protein	30.69 g.
Carbs	5.97 g.
Fat	13.76 g.

- In a large nonstick frying pan, heat oil over medium high heat and brown chicken on both sides. Remove chicken and place in a warm oven – about 250°.

- Reduce heat to medium and add butter and herbs to the pan. Sauté onions, peppers and mushrooms until soft, approximately 3 – 4 minutes.

- Add the chicken stock and wine and bring to a boil. Replace chicken in the pan and cover and simmer for approximately 5 minutes.

- Remove chicken and vegetables and set aside in a warm oven. Add heavy cream and fresh ground pepper. Bring to a vigorous boil, reduce heat and simmer for 3 – 4 minutes until liquid is reduced and sauce has thickened. You may need to add 1 teaspoon of cornstarch, dissolved in a small amount of water, to thicken the sauce.

- Return chicken and vegetables to the pan and continue simmering for 2 – 3 minutes, turning chicken to coat.

- Serve the chicken breasts and top with vegetables and cream sauce.

- Makes 4 servings.

Chicken & Mushroom Casserole

4 cups cooked chicken, cut into bite
sized pieces

2 cups sliced fresh mushrooms

2 teaspoons butter

1 cup toasted blanched almonds, whole
or slivered

2½ cups white sauce (see below)

½ cup shredded cheese, either Cheddar,
Swiss or Mozzarella

White Sauce

6 teaspoons butter

2 tablespoons flour

2½ cups light cream (half & half)

½ teaspoon salt

1 teaspoon fresh ground pepper

1 tablespoon fresh chopped parsley

Nutrition Information Per Serving	
Calories	516.62
Protein	30.15 g.
Carbs	11.12 g.
Fat	40.11 g.

- ❀ Preheat oven to 325°. Sauté the mushrooms in butter over medium heat until soft, approximately 4 – 5 minutes. Set aside.
- ❀ Put the cut up chicken, toasted almonds and mushrooms in a large bowl.
- ❀ White Sauce: In the top of a double boiler, over simmering water, melt butter and add flour. Stir till smooth and completely blended. Gradually add the light cream, stirring constantly to avoid any lumps. Add the salt, pepper and parsley. Cook over the simmering water until the white sauce has thickened, about 15 minutes, stirring almost constantly to avoid any lumps.

continued next page

Chicken & Mushroom Casserole cont.

⁂ Cool the sauce slightly and pour over the chicken mixture and blend well. Pour into a 2 quart casserole and bake covered for 35 minutes.

⁂ Remove cover and sprinkle with the shredded cheese and continue baking for 15 additional minutes, or until cheese is melted and browned. Serve immediately.

⁂ Makes 6 servings.

Tip: This casserole may be made 3 – 4 hours in advance up to the stage where the white sauce is mixed with the chicken mixture and poured into the casserole. You may then put it in the fridge until one hour before serving. It may take a few minutes longer in the oven because it was chilled.

Tip: I buy a 3 lb. rotisserie chicken at the supermarket to provide the cooked chicken. It allows a nice mix of light and dark meat, as well as saving time.

Note: This is an old family favorite that my mother used to make. She used to top it with buttered breadcrumbs, which doesn't work for low carb, however the cheese topping is a very nice variation.

Chicken Breasts with Vegetable Medley

4 boneless, skinless chicken breasts

2 tablespoons olive oil

1 medium onion, halved and sliced thinly

1 sweet red pepper, halved and sliced

2 garlic cloves, minced

1 cup chicken bouillon

12 – 16 asparagus spears cut into 2" pieces

2 medium zucchini, halved and cut into ½" pieces

1 teaspoon fresh ground pepper

½ teaspoon salt

½ teaspoon dried thyme, divided

1 tablespoon fresh chopped parsley to garnish

Nutrition Information Per Serving	
Calories	247.69
Protein	31.66 g.
Carbs	8.36 g.
Fat	9.04 g.

- ❀ Preheat oven to 375°.
- ❀ Season chicken breasts with salt, pepper and half the thyme.
- ❀ Heat oil in a large frying pan, over medium high heat. Add chicken and brown well on both sides, about 3 minutes a side.
- ❀ Remove chicken from pan and place in a casserole dish.
- ❀ Sauté garlic, onion, pepper and zucchini for 2 – 3 minutes, until just soft. Add the asparagus spears and continue cooking for 1 minute longer. Additional olive oil may be added if necessary.
- ❀ Add the chicken bouillon and bring to a boil. Season with additional pepper if desired, and the remaining thyme.
- ❀ Pour mixture over chicken in the casserole dish and bake, covered, for 20 – 25 minutes.
- ❀ Serve, distributing the vegetables evenly and garnish with the chopped parsley.
- ❀ Makes 4 servings.

Chicken with Creamy Mushroom Sauce

4 boneless, skinless chicken breasts

2 tablespoons butter

2 cups fresh mushrooms, cleaned & thinly sliced

1 cup heavy cream

½ teaspoon dried basil

½ teaspoon dried thyme

fresh ground pepper to taste

¼ teaspoon Fine Herbs

½ teaspoon cornstarch

1 additional teaspoon Fine Herbs

Nutrition Information Per Serving	
Calories	410.33
Protein	31.13 g.
Carbs	4.36 g.
Fat	29.56 g.

Tip: This is a rich, delicious dish, which is best served with a green salad and fresh asparagus or some other green vegetable.

❈ Trim any fat from chicken breasts. Place cleaned chicken breasts between waxed paper and pound with rolling pin until slightly flattened.

❈ Make a spice mixture using the basil, thyme, pepper and Fine Herbs. Sprinkle both sides of the chicken with the herb mixture.

❈ Melt 1 tablespoon of the butter in a medium hot frying pan. Add the chicken and brown on both sides, approximately 3 – 4 minutes a side, until the juices run clear. Remove the chicken to a baking dish, and place in a warm oven (250°).

❈ Add remaining tablespoon of butter to frying pan. Sauté mushrooms until tender, approximately 3 – 4 minutes.

❈ Reduce heat to medium and add the cream to the mushrooms and stir vigorously, loosening any brown spots at the bottom of the pan.

❈ Add salt and ground pepper to taste, with 1 teaspoon of Fine Herbs. Reduce heat and simmer for 2 – 3 minutes. Combine ¼ teaspoon cornstarch with a small amount of water and add to the sauce to thicken, while stirring constantly.

❈ Remove chicken from oven and place in the frying pan, for a minute or two, turning to coat with cream sauce.

❈ Serve chicken and spoon creamy mushroom sauce over each breast.

❈ Makes 4 servings.

Chicken with Citrus Cranberry Sauce

4 boneless, skinless chicken breasts
2 tablespoons olive oil
⅓ cup Low Carb Cranberry Sauce (see below)
1 tablespoon fresh chopped thyme
½ tablespoon fresh chopped parsley
fresh ground pepper and salt to taste
⅓ cup chicken bouillon
¼ cup fresh lemon juice
1½ tablespoons Dijon mustard
2 tablespoons heavy cream
1 tablespoon fresh chopped parsley

Low Carb Cranberry Sauce
1½ cups raw cranberries
¼ cup water
6 packets Splenda™
zest of small orange

Nutrition Information Per Serving	
Calories	244.41
Protein	30.56 g.
Carbs	4.79 g.
Fat	12.48 g.

- Bring all ingredients for the cranberry sauce to a boil over medium heat. Reduce heat and simmer for 5 minutes. Makes approximately 1 cup of tart cranberry sauce. Use only ⅓ cup in this recipe.
- Sprinkle chicken with thyme, parsley, salt and fresh ground pepper.
- Heat the oil in a heavy skillet over medium heat. Add chicken and brown well on both sides, approximately 3 – 4 minutes a side. Remove to an oven proof pan and place in a warm oven (250°).
- Add remaining ingredients to the skillet, stirring constantly to blend well, and bring to a boil. Reduce heat to medium and simmer for about 5 – 6 minutes until sauce thickens slightly.
- Return chicken to skillet, turning to coat, and simmer for an additional 5 minutes.
- Transfer chicken to plates and spoon Citrus Cranberry Sauce over.
- Makes 4 servings.

Chicken with Herbs & Balsamic Vinegar

4 boneless, skinless chicken breasts

2 tablespoons butter

salt and fresh ground pepper to taste

1 green onion, finely chopped

1 teaspoon each fresh chopped rosemary, thyme, parsley, chives & oregano

2 tablespoons olive oil

2 tablespoons balsamic vinegar

Nutrition Information Per Serving	
Calories	342.94
Protein	54.60 g.
Carbs	0.57 g.
Fat	11.91 g.

❀ Put olive oil in a small bowl and add fresh herbs. Set aside.

❀ Pound chicken breasts flat between two sheets of waxed paper. Salt and pepper breasts. Heat butter in a heavy frying pan over medium heat. Add chicken and sauté to brown on each side, approximately 4 minutes per side.

❀ Remove chicken from pan and place in a warm oven (250°).

❀ Reduce heat and put green onion in the frying pan. Sauté 2 – 3 minutes.

❀ Add herbs and vinegar to pan and continue cooking to reduce by half.

❀ Put chicken breasts on plates and top with herbs in vinegar.

❀ Makes 4 servings.

Chicken Roulade

4 boneless, skinless chicken breasts

8 large spinach leaves

1 small zucchini

1 small carrot

4 tablespoons butter, divided

1 teaspoon fresh chopped rosemary

1 teaspoon fresh chopped thyme

1 teaspoon fresh ground pepper

½ teaspoon salt

½ cup sherry

kitchen string

Nutrition Information Per Serving	
Calories	285.52
Protein	29.93 g.
Carbs	2.81 g.
Fat	13.13 g.

❀ Pound the chicken breasts flat, between two sheets of waxed paper. (I remove the little fillet on the side, which makes it easier to flatten the breast. I use my rolling pin to pound flat.) Set aside.

❀ Finely shred the zucchini and carrot and set aside.

❀ Wash the spinach leaves and cook in a sauce pan over high heat for 1 minute, using only the water that clings to the leaves. Remove from pan and place on a paper towel to drain.

❀ Put 2 tablespoons of the butter in a large frying pan and sauté the zucchini and carrot with salt, pepper and fresh herbs over medium heat for 3 – 4 minutes until soft.

❀ Lay the flattened chicken breasts on a clean sheet of wax paper, with smooth side down. Place two of the cooked spinach leaves on each breast, to cover the exposed side. Take a spoonful of the zucchini and carrot mixture, and smooth a thin layer over the spinach leaves.

continued next page

Chicken Roulade cont.

※ Slowly and carefully roll up each breast and tie together at each end with the kitchen string. At this point the chicken may be covered with clear wrap and put into the fridge until 20 minutes before serving, if desired. This can be done 2 – 3 hours ahead of time.

※ Put 2 tablespoons of butter into a large frying pan over medium high heat, and brown rolled chicken on all sides (4 - 6 minutes). Add the sherry and bring to a boil. Reduce heat, cover pan and simmer chicken for 15 minutes, turning once.

※ Remove chicken from frying pan to a cutting board. Remove the string and cut each breast into 3 slices.

※ Serve the chicken in overlapping slices on each plate. This is extremely pleasing to the eye, with the chicken, green spinach, and orange filling in the center.

※ Makes 4 servings.

Note: Although this is a little fussy, it is not difficult and it is very attractive and tasty. I serve it on special occasions, because it looks so appealing.

Note: Thanks to my friend Caroline Thoma, who suggested the name for this dish.

Chicken with Lemon and Mint

4 boneless, skinless chicken breasts

1 teaspoon lemon zest

¼ cup lemon juice

1 tablespoon olive oil

2 cloves garlic, minced

2 tablespoons fresh chopped mint

1 tablespoon fresh chopped thyme

½ teaspoon ground cumin

Nutrition Information Per Serving	
Calories	246.88
Protein	29.35 g.
Carbs	2.37 g.
Fat	12.31 g.

❊ Remove any fat from chicken breasts and place in a shallow baking dish.

❊ Blend lemon juice, zest, olive oil and herbs together in a small bowl. Pour over chicken and turn chicken to coat. Marinate in fridge for one hour.

❊ Heat grill to medium and place chicken on grill. Cook for 5 – 6 minutes per side, depending on thickness, until juices run clear.

❊ Makes 4 servings.

Chicken Stew

2 – 3 lb. whole chicken, cut up

2 tablespoons olive oil

2 sprigs each fresh thyme, rosemary & oregano

3 cups chicken bouillon

12 – 16 pearl onions

2 medium carrots

8 celery sticks, leafy tops included

1 small turnip

2 teaspoons dried thyme

1 tablespoon flour

salt & fresh ground pepper to taste

Nutrition Information Per Serving	
Calories	348.12
Protein	26.15 g.
Carbs	4.43 g.
Fat	24.28 g.

- ❀ Preheat oven to 350°
- ❀ In a deep 4 quart casserole, heat oil over medium heat. Salt & pepper chicken pieces and sprinkle with dried thyme. Brown chicken pieces in hot oil, on all sides. Remove from casserole and set aside.
- ❀ Sauté pearl onions for 2 – 3 minutes. Put chicken back in casserole, add the chicken bouillon and the leafy tops only of the celery. Bring to a boil on the stove top and then place in the oven for 2 hours.
- ❀ One hour before serving, remove casserole from oven and add carrot and turnip cut into bite sized pieces. Remove celery leafy tops, and add celery sticks cut into 2" pieces.
- ❀ Add additional chicken bouillon if the stew seems dry or liquid does not cover all vegetables at this point. Mix the tablespoon of flour with 3 tablespoons of water to dissolve, and add to the stew stirring well to distribute. (This will thicken the sauce.)
- ❀ Replace in the oven for final hour of cooking.
- ❀ Serve chicken pieces with vegetables and sauce on each plate.
- ❀ Makes 6 – 8 servings.

Chicken Tenders

4 boneless, skinless chicken breasts, cut into ½" strips

2 tablespoons olive oil

¼ cup fine bread crumbs

1 tablespoon flour

¼ teaspoon cayenne

1 teaspoon lemon pepper

¼ teaspoon paprika

1 teaspoon thyme

½ teaspoon salt

Nutrition Information Per Serving / Chicken	
Calories	242.82
Protein	30.17 g.
Carbs	7.09 g.
Fat	9.01 g.

❀ Preheat oven to 375°.

❀ Combine bread crumbs and spices in a small bowl and mix well.

❀ Put cut chicken pieces into a large bowl. Drizzle with the olive oil and stir to coat well. Sprinkle the spice mixture over the chicken and mix well to coat thoroughly.

❀ Place chicken on a cookie sheet that has been sprayed with a no-stick agent. Sprinkle any remaining spices on the chicken.

❀ Bake for 18 – 20 minutes, turning once. The chicken should be nicely browned.

❀ Serve with the mustard dipping sauce.

❀ Makes 6 servings.

Mustard Dipping Sauce

2 tablespoon Dijon mustard

1 teaspoon mayonnaise

2 packets Splenda™

1 teaspoon white wine vinegar

Nutrition Information Per Serving / Sauce	
Calories	12.28
Protein	1.00 g.
Carbs	1.37 g.
Fat	1.61 g.

❀ Whisk together all ingredients until smooth.

❀ Serve in small individual dishes for dipping.

Coq au Vin

3 lb. roasting chicken, cut up
2 tablespoons butter
6 slices bacon, diced
8 – 10 whole small mushrooms
12 – 16 pearl onions, peeled
½ cup sliced green onion
1 clove garlic, finely minced
3 celery tops with leaves
1½ tablespoons flour
1 teaspoon salt
1 teaspoon fresh ground pepper
1 teaspoon dried thyme
2 cups chicken bouillon
1 cup white wine

Nutrition Information Per Serving	
Calories	550.29
Protein	41.13 g.
Carbs	7.65 g.
Fat	36.23 g.

Note: The pearl onions are a bit fussy, but well worth the effort in terms of taste and presentation.

- ❀ Clean and pat dry chicken pieces.
- ❀ In a Dutch oven, over medium heat, sauté bacon until crisp and remove from pan. Add butter to bacon drippings in pan and brown chicken well on all sides. Remove chicken from pan and set aside.
- ❀ Pour off all but 2 tablespoons of the fat and add mushrooms and onions and cook until tender and browned. Remove from pan. Add garlic and sauté for 2 – 3 minutes.
- ❀ Remove pan from heat and add flour, salt, pepper and thyme. Return pan to heat and cook stirring constantly until flour is browned, about 3 minutes.
- ❀ Gradually add the chicken bouillon and wine, stirring constantly. Bring mixture to a boil.
- ❀ Remove from heat and add bacon, mushrooms and onions, chicken and celery stalks. Let cool and place in the fridge for 2 – 3 hours.
- ❀ Preheat oven to 400°. Bake chicken in covered Dutch oven for approximately 1½ to 2 hours until chicken is tender but not falling apart. Remove celery sticks before serving.
- ❀ Makes 8 servings.

Crispy Oven Baked Chicken

4 chicken breasts (bone in and skin on)

3 tablespoons Crisco cooking oil

1 teaspoon Lawry's Seasoned Salt

1 teaspoon fresh ground pepper

1 teaspoon Fine Herbs

½ teaspoon paprika

Nutrition Information Per Serving	
Calories	366.01
Protein	33.14 g.
Carbs	0.52 g.
Fat	24.68 g.

- ❈ Preheat oven to 400°.
- ❈ Combine cooking oil and seasonings in a small bowl. Clean and pat dry chicken breasts. Brush both sides of chicken breasts with the oil mixture.
- ❈ Place chicken breasts, skin side up, in a baking dish sprayed with a no stick agent.
- ❈ Bake for 45 – 55 minutes, depending on the thickness of the breasts, until skin is browned and crispy and the juices run clear when pierced.
- ❈ Makes 4 servings.

Note: My cousin Margot Tompkins gets credit for this easy and delicious recipe, which tastes like fried chicken with none of the hassle of deep-frying.

Tip: This recipe can be made with other chicken parts, including legs, thighs and wings, with an adjustment in the baking time according to the portion sizes.

Curried Chicken

4 boneless, skinless chicken breasts, cut
into 1" pieces
3 tablespoons olive oil
¼ teaspoon mustard seeds
¼ teaspoon cumin seeds
2 teaspoons curry powder
1 medium onion, thinly sliced
2 cloves garlic, minced
1, 14 oz. can of coconut milk
½ cup trimmed green beans
½ cup unsalted whole cashews

Nutrition Information Per Serving	
Calories	368.61
Protein	32.81 g.
Carbs	11.24 g.
Fat	20.99 g.

- ❋ Cut the beans into 1" pieces and cook with water in the microwave for 2 minutes. Remove from water and set aside.
- ❋ In a large nonstick frying pan, heat the olive oil over medium heat. Add the cut up chicken and brown on all sides. This will take 5 – 7 minutes. Remove chicken to an oven-proof dish and keep in a warm oven (250°).
- ❋ Put the garlic, mustard seed, cumin seed, curry powder and parsley in the frying pan and sauté for 2 – 3 minutes. Add the sliced onion and continue cooking until the onion is soft, about 3 – 4 minutes.
- ❋ Stir in the coconut milk and bring to a boil. Reduce heat and add the chicken, cashews and green beans to the pan. Cook until sauce thickens and chicken and beans are warmed through. You may need to add a teaspoon of cornstarch, dissolved in a small amount of water, to thicken the sauce.
- ❋ Serve over a bed of cooked thinly sliced green cabbage.
- ❋ Makes 4 servings.

Tip: This is a fairly light curry. To increase the flavor, simply increase the amount of curry powder.

Grilled Herb Chicken

4 boneless, skinless chicken breasts

3 tablespoons fresh lemon juice

3 tablespoons olive oil

2 tablespoons fresh chopped oregano

1 tablespoon fresh chopped parsley

1 tablespoon fresh chopped chives

1 teaspoon fresh ground pepper

½ teaspoon salt

½ teaspoon paprika

Nutrition Information Per Serving	
Calories	240.19
Protein	29.31 g.
Carbs	2.35 g.
Fat	12.17 g.

❈ Whisk together olive oil, lemon juice, oregano, parsley, chives, paprika and salt and pepper. Pour over chicken in a shallow bowl and turn to coat. Let stand for 30 – 45 minutes in the fridge.

❈ Heat grill to medium high heat. Place chicken on grill and close lid. Cook for 4 – 5 minutes on each side until juices run clear and chicken is cooked through. The cooking time will vary with the size and thickness of the chicken breasts.

❈ Makes 4 servings.

Lemon Herb Chicken

4 boneless, skinless chicken breasts

Lemon Herb Marinade

¼ cup olive oil

2 tablespoons lemon juice

1 teaspoon Fine Herbs

1 teaspoon dried thyme

1 teaspoon dried rosemary

pinch of salt

fresh ground pepper to taste

Nutrition Information Per Serving	
Calories	268.07
Protein	29.24 g.
Carbs	1.41 g.
Fat	15.65 g.

- ❀ Cut any fat off chicken breasts and pat dry.
- ❀ Whisk together ingredients for marinade and pour over chicken in shallow bowl. Turn to coat and let stand in the fridge for one hour.
- ❀ Heat grill or BBQ to medium high. Grill chicken breasts for 4 – 5 minutes a side until juices run clear.
- ❀ Makes 4 servings.

Lemon Thyme Chicken

4 boneless, skinless chicken breasts

¼ cup lemon juice

1 tablespoon fresh chopped thyme

½ tablespoon fresh chopped rosemary

1 tablespoon Dijon mustard

1 teaspoon fresh ground pepper

½ teaspoon salt

Nutrition Information Per Serving	
Calories	151.20
Protein	29.44 g.
Carbs	2.21 g.
Fat	1.81 g.

❀ Whisk together mustard, lemon juice, rosemary, thyme and salt and pepper. Pour over chicken in a shallow bowl and turn to coat. Let stand for 15 minutes.

❀ Heat grill to medium high heat. Place chicken on grill and close lid. Cook for 4 – 5 minutes on each side until juices run clear and chicken is cooked through. Cooking time will vary with the size and thickness of the chicken breasts.

❀ Makes 4 servings.

Orange Chicken

4 boneless, skinless chicken breasts

Orange Marinade

¼ cup fresh orange juice
(juice of small orange)

1 tablespoon orange zest

2 tablespoons olive oil

4 teaspoons soy sauce

Nutrition Information Per Serving	
Calories	213.18
Protein	29.87 g.
Carbs	2.19 g.
Fat	8.62 g.

❀ Whisk together ingredients for orange marinade. Pour over chicken breasts in a shallow bowl, and turn to coat. Marinate in the fridge for an hour.

❀ Preheat grill to medium high. Place marinated breasts on grill and cook for 4 – 5 minutes a side until done. This recipe may also be done in a frying pan, and will usually take just a bit longer to cook using this method.

❀ Makes 4 servings.

Note: Thanks to my friend Sarah Smith for sharing the basic ingredients of this great marinade.

Pecan Chicken with Dijon Sauce

4 boneless, skinless chicken breasts

2 tablespoons olive oil

¾ cup finely chopped pecans

1 tablespoon fresh chopped thyme

2 tablespoons fresh chopped parsley

1 teaspoon fresh ground pepper

½ teaspoon salt

½ teaspoon cayenne

½ teaspoon dry mustard

1 egg

Dijon Sauce

½ cup sour cream

2 tablespoons grainy Dijon mustard

pinch of salt

Nutrition Information Per Serving	
Calories	429.75
Protein	31.76 g.
Carbs	6.23 g.
Fat	30.48 g.

- ❀ Whisk together, in a shallow bowl, pecans, parsley, thyme, salt, cayenne, and dry mustard. Set aside.
- ❀ In a separate bowl, beat egg.
- ❀ Pound chicken breast flat with a rolling pin, between sheets of wax paper, until half normal thickness.
- ❀ Dip each chicken breast in the beaten egg and then in the pecan mixture, coating both sides and pressing into the chicken.
- ❀ Heat oil over medium high heat in a heavy non-stick skillet. Cook chicken, turning once, for approximately 10 – 12 minutes until no longer pink inside. If nuts start to get too brown, reduce heat and cook for a few minutes longer.
- ❀ In a small bowl, mix sour cream, mustard and salt to make sauce. Serve sauce on the side.
- ❀ Makes 4 servings.

Roast Chicken with Lemon & Rosemary

1 whole roasting chicken, about 3 lbs.

1 tablespoon olive oil

2 wedges of fresh lemon

4 sprigs fresh rosemary

4 sprigs fresh oregano

4 sprigs fresh lemon thyme

1 teaspoon dried rosemary

1 teaspoon dried thyme

Nutrition Information Per Serving	
Calories	387.91
Protein	61.39 g.
Carbs	0.48 g.
Fat	13.34 g.

※ Preheat oven to 350°. Clean and pat dry chicken.

※ Put lemon wedges and 2 sprigs each of the fresh herbs in the chicken cavity.

※ Baste the skin with olive oil and sprinkle the dried herbs over the chicken. Tuck remaining fresh herbs around the wings and legs.

※ Roast the chicken for 2½ hours, (using ¾ hour per pound due to lemon wedges in cavity) or longer depending on size. Remove from oven and remove all fresh herbs and lemon wedges before carving.

※ Makes 6 – 8 servings.

Spicy Chicken Wings

2 lbs. chicken wings or drumettes

2 tablespoons olive oil

2 teaspoons Lawry's seasoned salt

2 teaspoons citrus & pepper seasoning

1 teaspoon paprika

1 teaspoon cayenne

1 teaspoon ground thyme

Nutrition Information Per Serving	
Calories	467.25
Protein	61.65.g.
Carbs	1.70 g.
Fat	22.17 g.

❀ Wash and pat dry chicken wings or drumettes and place in bowl.

❀ Pour olive oil over chicken and toss to coat thoroughly.

❀ Blend all spices together in small dish and then sprinkle over chicken parts and toss to coat. Use hands to rub spices into chicken skin.

❀ Place on a medium grill and grill 6 – 7 minutes a side until desired doneness. This chicken may also be baked in a hot oven (375°), for approximately 20 minutes, turning after 10 minutes.

❀ Makes 4 servings, as a meal.

Tip: You may want to use Mustard Dipping Sauce, found with Chicken Tenders, to dip the spicy wings.

Note: This is one of two recipes inspired by my daughter-in-law, Sian Haakonson.

Turkey/Beef Burgers

½ pound lean ground turkey

½ pound lean ground beef

4 tablespoons minced red onion

2 cloves garlic, minced

1 egg

1 teaspoon tomato paste

1 teaspoon Worcestershire sauce

½ teaspoon paprika

½ teaspoon cayenne

¼ teaspoon ground cumin

salt & fresh ground pepper to taste

Nutrition Information Per Serving	
Calories	279.65
Protein	28.53 g.
Carbs	3.58 g.
Fat	16.38 g.

- ❁ Combine beef and turkey in a large bowl.
- ❁ In a separate bowl, combine the egg with tomato paste, Worcestershire sauce and spices.
- ❁ Add the onion, garlic and egg mixture to the meat. Blend well.
- ❁ Divide into 4 portions and form patties.
- ❁ Place on a hot grill and cook 4 – 5 minutes on each side, for well done, or until desired doneness.
- ❁ You may baste with BBQ sauce, if desired. This will increase carbohydrates.
- ❁ Makes 4 servings.

Turkey Burgers

1 lb. ground turkey

1 tablespoon minced fresh thyme

½ tablespoon minced fresh rosemary

1 tablespoon minced fresh parsley

1 tablespoon minced fresh chives

1 small egg, slightly beaten

¼ cup fine bread crumbs

¼ cup chopped green onion

1 teaspoon fresh ground pepper

½ teaspoon salt

Nutrition Information Per Serving	
Calories	221.35
Protein	22.78 g.
Carbs	6.46 g.
Fat	11.10 g.

- ❁ Combine all ingredients in a bowl and mix well. Divide into four portions and make patties.
- ❁ Preheat grill to medium high. Place burgers on grill and cook 6 – 7 minutes a side until done through.
- ❁ Makes 4 servings.

Turkey Loaf

1½ lbs. ground turkey (½ breast meat & ½ thigh)

¼ cup fine bread crumbs

1 egg, slightly beaten

⅓ cup red onion, minced

½ cup celery, minced

2 medium mushrooms, minced

½ cup chicken bouillon

1 teaspoon Fine Herbs

salt & fresh ground pepper to taste

Nutrition Information Per Serving	
Calories	207.57
Protein	21.98 g.
Carbs	4.87 g.
Fat	10.66 g.

- ❈ Preheat oven to 350°.
- ❈ Mix all ingredients in a large bowl. Place into loaf pan and press with spoon. Sprinkle top with additional ½ teaspoon Fine Herbs and cover with foil.
- ❈ Bake for 55 minutes and remove foil. Bake an additional 5 minutes.
- ❈ Makes 6 servings.

Note: This loaf is somewhat pale in color, but very tasty. You may wish to add some Low Carb Cranberry Sauce as a garnish, but this will slightly increase the carbohydrates.

FISH

~

Baked Sole

4 fillets of sole (4 – 6 oz. each)

⅓ cup fine bread crumbs

1 teaspoon paprika

½ teaspoon each basil, thyme, oregano, rosemary

¼ teaspoon cayenne pepper

1 teaspoon fresh ground pepper

⅓ cup whole milk

4 sprigs fresh parsley

4 lemon wedges

Nutrition Information Per Serving	
Calories	187.93
Protein	30.46 g.
Carbs	8.33 g.
Fat	2.81 g.

❧ Preheat oven to 350°.

❧ Mix spices together with bread crumbs in a shallow bowl.

❧ Dip fillets in whole milk and then coat with seasoned bread crumbs.

❧ Place fillets in a baking dish that has been sprayed with a no stick agent. Bake for 10 –15 minutes depending on the thickness of the fillets. To test for doneness, use a fork and fish will flake easily and will be opaque throughout when done.

❧ Serve with a lemon wedge and a sprig of fresh parsley.

❧ Makes 4 servings.

Baked Whole Salmon

1, 2 – 3 lb. dressed salmon

4 thin lemon slices

4 thin onion rings

1 tablespoon fresh chopped parsley

½ tablespoon fresh chopped rosemary

¼ cup fresh lemon juice

2 teaspoons butter

fresh ground pepper and salt to taste

Nutrition Information Per Serving	
Calories	219.59
Protein	22.66 g.
Carbs	4.32 g.
Fat	13.08 g.

- ❀ Preheat oven to 400°. Spray a large baking dish with a no-stick product.
- ❀ Salmon should have head removed and interior cavity cleaned. Wash with cold water and pat dry.
- ❀ Open the cavity and place layers of lemon slices, onion slices, fresh herbs, salt and pepper inside. Dot with small amounts of butter.
- ❀ Place the salmon in the baking dish and sprinkle with lemon juice. Pour remaining juice in the bottom of the baking dish.
- ❀ Bake uncovered for 20 – 25 minutes, allowing approximately 9 – 10 minutes / per lb., depending on the thickness of the fish. Test with a fork for doneness, fish should be evenly pink throughout and flake easily.
- ❀ To serve, remove skin and cut sections of fish on either side of the back bone. Serve with a wedge of lemon.
- ❀ Makes 8 – 12 servings.

Note: This fish presents very well, since it is cooked whole. I often bring it to the table on a pretty platter to serve.

Broiled Halibut

4 halibut steaks, about 1½" thick
(4 – 6 oz. each)

2 teaspoons butter

2 teaspoons lemon juice

2 teaspoons fresh chopped thyme

1 tablespoon fresh chopped parsley

salt & fresh ground pepper to taste

4 lemon wedges

Nutrition Information Per Serving	
Calories	146.47
Protein	23.92 g.
Carbs	1.20 g.
Fat	4.58 g.

❀ Preheat broiler for 10 minutes.

❀ Rinse halibut under cold water and pat dry. Place on rack of broiler pan that has been sprayed with no stick product.

❀ Sprinkle with herbs, salt and pepper. Distribute butter evenly in little pats, and sprinkle with lemon juice.

❀ Place pan 2" from broiler and broil for 5 – 6 minutes a side or until fish is no longer opaque and flakes easily with a fork. The broiling time will vary with the thickness of the steaks. Be sure to test for doneness before removing from oven.

❀ *To Finish:* Serve with a fresh lemon wedge and additional fresh chopped parsley sprinkled on the halibut.

❀ Makes 4 servings

Tip: Although fresh herbs make a difference in taste and presentation, dried herbs may be used and quantities should be halved in this case.

Broiled Salmon

4 salmon fillets (about 4-6 oz. each)

2 teaspoons lemon juice

1 teaspoon butter

1 tablespoon each fresh chopped thyme,
parsley, chives

1 teaspoon fresh ground pepper

Nutrition Information Per Serving	
Calories	253.48
Protein	33.87 g.
Carbs	0.68 g.
Fat	11.81 g.

❈ Preheat broiler. Spray broiler rack with non-stick agent.

❈ Place fillets on broiler pan and sprinkle each fillet with the combined fresh herbs. Put a dot of butter on each fillet and sprinkle with lemon juice.

❈ Place broiler pan 2" from broiler and broil for 7 – 10 minutes, without turning, until cooked through. Test for doneness with fork and fish should flake easily and be pink throughout.

❈ Serve with a lemon wedge.

❈ Makes 4 servings.

Cold Salmon with Dill Sauce

1½ lb. salmon fillet

½ cup white wine

¼ cup fresh lemon juice

1 tablespoon fresh chopped parsley

1 teaspoon fresh ground pepper

Nutrition Information Per Serving	
Calories	323.86
Protein	22.65 g.
Carbs	3.13 g.
Fat	23.19 g.

Dill Sauce

⅓ cup mayonnaise

2 teaspoons fresh lemon juice

1 packet Splenda™

1 tablespoon fresh chopped dill

- ❀ Place all Dill Sauce ingredients in a small bowl and whisk to blend until smooth. Keep refrigerated until ready to serve.
- ❀ Preheat oven to 400°. Spray baking pan with no stick agent.
- ❀ Place salmon in the baking dish (skin down if skin attached). Sprinkle the salmon with the fresh ground pepper and parsley. Add the white wine and lemon juice to the bottom of the pan. Cover the pan with foil and seal the edges.
- ❀ Bake for 15 – 20 minutes until the fish is cooked through. The fish will flake easily and be a uniform pink throughout when done. Cooking time may vary, depending on the thickness of the fish.
- ❀ Let cool slightly, and remove from the pan and chill in the fridge for at least 2 – 3 hours. Serve with Dill Sauce on the side.
- ❀ Makes 4 – 6 servings.

Grilled Halibut

4 halibut steaks, about 1" thick

3 lemons

2 tablespoons olive oil

2 teaspoons fresh chopped oregano

1 teaspoon fresh chopped chives

1 teaspoon fresh chopped rosemary

1 teaspoon fresh chopped parsley

salt & fresh ground pepper to taste

Nutrition Information Per Serving	
Calories	265
Protein	36.41 g.
Carbs	6.49 g.
Fat	11.20 g.

- In a small bowl, combine zest of one lemon and juice of two lemons with olive oil and fresh herbs.
- Rinse halibut under cold water and pat dry. Place in a shallow dish.
- Pour lemon juice and herb marinade over halibut and marinate in fridge for 1 hour.
- Heat grill to medium. Spray a grilling basket with a no-stick product. Place halibut steaks in grilling basket and grill for 3 – 4 minutes a side or until fish is no longer opaque and flakes easily with a fork. The grilling time will vary with the thickness of the steaks.
- *To Finish:* Serve with a fresh lemon wedge and additional fresh chopped parsley sprinkled on the halibut.
- If available, a small mound of cooked sea asparagus (found in the fresh fish department) on each steak makes a dramatic garnish.
- Makes 4 servings.

Tip: Although fresh herbs make a difference in taste and appearance, dried herbs may be used and quantities should be halved in this case.

Salmon Poached with Vegetables

4 salmon fillets (about 4 – 6 oz. each)
or steaks about 1" thick

⅔ cup chicken bouillon

1 cup green beans, trimmed
(or fresh asparagus)

½ cup julienne carrots

6 sprigs of fresh thyme

1 clove of garlic, minced

1 cup julienne yellow or green zucchini,

or ½ cup each, matchstick cut red &
green pepper

⅔ cup white wine

salt & fresh ground pepper to taste

Nutrition Information Per Serving	
Calories	295
Protein	35.38 g.
Carbs	11.63 g.
Fat	29.26 g.

✹ Wash all vegetables well and prepare according to ingredient list.

✹ Preheat oven to 350°.

✹ In a stove top and oven safe casserole, combine chicken bouillon, green beans, carrots, thyme and garlic. Bring to a simmer over medium heat, cover and cook for 5 minutes. Stir in either zucchini or bell peppers and wine. Simmer for 1 minute and remove from heat.

✹ Season salmon with salt and pepper. Place salmon over vegetables in pan (if using fillets, place skin side up).

✹ Cover with lid and bake at 350° for 10 – 15 minutes, depending on thickness of fish. Fish is done when it flakes easily with fork and is a uniform pink throughout.

✹ Discard thyme sprigs. Serve salmon and vegetables on individual plates and garnish with lemon wedge and fresh chopped parsley. Drizzle with cooking liquid.

✹ Makes 4 servings.

Salmon Poached in White Wine

1½ lb. salmon fillet

⅓ cup white wine

⅓ cup fresh lemon juice

4 thin lemon slices

4 rounds of sweet onion, thinly sliced

1 tablespoon each fresh chopped
rosemary, thyme, parsley

Lemon Thyme Sauce (see next page)

Nutrition Information Per Serving	
Calories	285.00
Protein	28.42 g.
Carbs	2.71 g.
Fat	15.41 g.

❀ Preheat oven to 400°. Spray baking pan with no stick agent. You may have a single large piece of fish, or 4 individual fillets – the recipe works either way.

❀ Place salmon in the baking dish (skin down if skin attached). Layer the salmon with the fresh herbs, the sliced lemon and the sliced onion. Add the white wine and lemon juice to the bottom of the pan. Cover the pan with foil and seal the edges.

❀ Bake for 15 – 20 minutes until the fish is cooked through. The fish will flake easily and be a uniform pink throughout when done.

❀ Serve with Lemon Thyme Sauce on the side.

❀ Makes 4 servings.

Tip: I usually do more salmon than I need when using this recipe, because the salmon is so moist. The next day I make salmon salad with the leftovers.

Lemon Thyme Sauce

1 tablespoon butter

juice of 1 lemon

1 teaspoon of lemon zest

1 tablespoon each fresh chopped thyme
& parsley

½ tablespoon fresh chopped rosemary

½ cup heavy cream

1 teaspoon cornstarch

½ teaspoon salt

Nutrition Information Per Serving	
Calories	90.46
Protein	0.52 g.
Carbs	1.98 g.
Fat	9.32 g.

※ Melt butter over medium heat in a small saucepan. Add herbs and sauté for 2 minutes, stirring constantly. Add the juice and zest of the lemon.

※ Gradually add the heavy cream and cornstarch. (Dissolve cornstarch in a small amount of water before adding to the sauce.) Add the salt.

※ Simmer for 5 – 6 minutes, while stirring constantly, until the sauce thickens. Serve warm from a gravy dish or other serving dish.

※ Makes 4 – 6 servings.

Note: If the sauce is a bit tart, add additional salt to taste, to diminish the tartness. This sauce may be made 2 – 3 hours ahead of time, kept in the fridge and reheated gently over a slow element.

Salmon with Citrus Sauce

4 salmon fillets (about 4 – 6 oz. each)

2 teaspoons butter

½ teaspoon salt

½ teaspoon fresh ground pepper

Citrus Sauce

2 tablespoons finely minced onion

¼ cup white wine

¼ cup fresh orange juice

1 tablespoon balsamic vinegar

1 teaspoon butter

1 teaspoon orange zest

1 teaspoon each fresh chopped mint & thyme

2 teaspoons fresh chopped parsley

Nutrition Information Per Serving	
Calories	207.90
Protein	22.68 g.
Carbs	1.90 g.
Fat	10.12 g.

- ❀ Preheat oven to 450°. Spray a baking pan with a no-stick agent.
- ❀ Season the salmon with salt and pepper. Melt 2 teaspoons of butter in a large frying pan over medium high heat, and brown the fillets on both sides. This will take 3 minutes or so, each side.
- ❀ Place the salmon in the baking dish. Bake for 7 – 10 minutes until the fish is cooked through. The fish will flake easily and be a uniform pink throughout when done.
- ❀ While the fish is baking, proceed with the Citrus Sauce. Place the wine, balsamic vinegar and orange juice in a small saucepan. Bring to a boil, add the chopped onion and simmer for 3 – 4 minutes until slightly thickened.
- ❀ Remove from heat and add the butter, orange zest and herbs, stirring constantly.
- ❀ Remove salmon fillets from oven, place on individual plates, and serve sauce over the salmon.
- ❀ Makes 4 servings.

Sole with Herb Butter

4 fillets of sole (4 – 6 oz. each)

1 tablespoon olive oil

2 tablespoons butter

½ tablespoon each fresh chopped dill, thyme, mint

1 tablespoon fresh chopped parsley

1 teaspoon fresh ground pepper

½ teaspoon salt

¼ cup whole milk

4 sprigs fresh parsley, or dill

4 lemon wedges

Nutrition Information Per Serving	
Calories	229.61
Protein	29.18 g.
Carbs	1.63 g.
Fat	11.34 g.

❀ Bring butter to room temperature. Add lemon juice and fresh chopped herbs and mix well with a fork until blended. Form small swirls or patties with the butter and place on waxed paper and put in the fridge to chill.

❀ Dip fillets in whole milk. Heat olive oil in a large frying pan over medium high heat. Sprinkle fillets with fresh ground pepper and salt.

❀ Place fillets in frying pan and cook for 3 – 4 minutes a side until well browned and cooked through. To test for doneness, use a fork and fish will flake easily and will be opaque throughout when done.

❀ Serve with a pat of herb butter melting on the fillet, a lemon wedge and a sprig of fresh parsley or dill.

❀ Makes 4 servings.

Sole with Herbs & Spices

4 sole fillets (about 1½ lbs.)

⅓ cup fine bread crumbs

1 tablespoon flour

¾ teaspoon cayenne

1 teaspoon oregano

1½ teaspoons lemon pepper

½ teaspoon thyme

1 egg, slightly beaten

1 tablespoon olive oil

2 teaspoons freshly chopped parsley

Nutrition Information Per Serving	
Calories	235.53
Protein	31.78 g.
Carbs	9.30 g.
Fat	6.91 g.

❁ In a shallow dish, mix together the bread crumbs with all the spices and herbs, except the freshly chopped parsley.

❁ Dip the fillets in the egg mixture. Coat each fillet with the spice mixture on each side.

❁ Heat the olive oil in a medium hot skillet and add the fillets. Sauté for 3 – 4 minutes on each side, depending on thickness of fillets. Fish is done when browned and the meat flakes when a fork is inserted.

❁ Serve with lemon wedges and sprinkle each fillet with the fresh chopped parsley.

❁ Makes 4 servings.

Steamed Halibut with Herbs & Vegetables

4, 4 – 6 oz. halibut fillets

3 cups fresh broccoli florets

1 medium carrot, julienned

4 slices of thinly sliced onion

2 tablespoons water

2 tablespoons white wine

4 sprigs fresh lemon thyme

4 sprigs fresh parsley

1 teaspoon fresh ground pepper

4 slices lemon

4 wedges lemon

Nutrition Information Per Serving	
Calories	181.28
Protein	26.24 g.
Carbs	7.38 g.
Fat	2.95 g.

❀ Preheat oven to 450°. Place halibut in a no stick baking dish. Season with fresh ground pepper and layer with onion slice, lemon slice, sprigs of fresh herbs and carrot pieces. Place broccoli florets in middle of dish and add liquid.

❀ Cover the baking dish with aluminum foil and bake for 10 – 12 minutes. Test for doneness with a fork. Fish should be white and flaky when done.

❀ To serve, place fish on plates, removing lemon slice and herb sprigs. Spoon pan juices over halibut. Add vegetables and a wedge of fresh lemon.

❀ Makes 4 servings.

MEATS

Beef Burgers with Onions & Mushrooms

1 lb. lean ground beef

2 teaspoons olive oil

1 medium sweet onion, sliced and separated into rings

1 cup thinly sliced fresh mushrooms

2 teaspoons balsamic vinegar

½ teaspoon salt

1 teaspoon dried thyme

1½ teaspoons paprika

½ teaspoon cayenne

1 teaspoon ground pepper to taste

Nutrition Information Per Serving	
Calories	296.12
Protein	21.84 g.
Carbs	2.86 g.
Fat	21.32 g.

❀ Preheat grill to medium high heat.

❀ Combine all spices in a small bowl. Divide meat into four portions and form patties. Coat each side of the patty with spice mixture and press lightly with palms to ensure that spices stick to the patty.

❀ Place patties on grill and cook over medium high heat 4 – 5 minutes a side, depending on the thickness of the patty. Test for doneness. Burgers should be cooked through.

❀ While burgers are cooking, heat oil in a large frying pan over medium heat and add onions. Sauté onions until soft, about 3 minutes. Add mushrooms and cook for 5 minutes more, stirring constantly. Add vinegar to the pan and continue cooking for 2 minutes, stirring constantly. Remove from heat and set aside.

❀ Remove patties from grill and top with equal portions of the onion and mushroom mixture.

❀ Makes 4 servings.

Beef Bourguignon

1½ – 2 lbs. lean stewing beef

1 tablespoon butter

1 tablespoon olive oil

4 slices bacon, cut into ½" pieces

1½ cups beef bouillon

1 tablespoon flour

4 celery stick tops, including leaves

2 teaspoons Fine Herbs

salt & fresh ground pepper to taste

Nutrition Information Per Serving	
Calories	342.67
Protein	30.11 g.
Carbs	4.21 g.
Fat	22.47 g.

To Finish

1½ cups small fresh mushrooms, stems removed

½ cup pearl onions, peeled and washed

1 tablespoon butter

¼ cup red wine

❀ Preheat oven to 325°.

❀ Cut beef into bite sized pieces, and remove any fat. Season meat with salt and pepper.

❀ In a large oven and stove-top proof casserole, heat butter and olive oil over medium heat. Add beef and brown on all sides while stirring constantly. Remove beef from casserole and set aside.

❀ Add bacon to the casserole, and cook until crisp; approximately 2 – 3 minutes. Reduce heat and stir in the flour, making sure to loosen any brown bits from the bottom.

continued next page

Beef Bourguignon cont.

⚜ Add beef bouillon, celery tops, Fine Herbs and beef. Place casserole in the oven and simmer at 325° for 2 hours. (Check the casserole, and stir after one hour. Add additional beef bouillon if the dish is getting dry.)

To Finish

⚜ Approximately 35 minutes before serving, remove casserole from oven and remove celery tops and discard.

⚜ Sauté small mushrooms and pearl onions in butter in a frying pan for 2 – 3 minutes. Add red wine and bring to a boil.

⚜ Add wine with vegetables to casserole and return to the oven to continue simmering for 30 minutes.

⚜ Makes 6 servings.

Note: The pearl onions are fussy to peel, but are worth the trouble.

BBQ Spare Ribs

2 racks of pork (or beef) back ribs
(about 2-3 lbs.)

1 small onion, halved

4 cups chicken bouillon

4 celery stalks with leaves on

fresh ground pepper and salt to taste

BBQ Sauce – see next page

Nutrition Information Per Serving – Ribs only	
Calories	405.15
Protein	26.56 g.
Carbs	0.00 g.
Fat	32.39 g.

- ❈ Cut ribs into sections of 3 – 4 bones each. Salt and pepper the ribs.
- ❈ Fill large stock pot or stew pot with bouillon and add enough water to ½ full. Put ribs, onion, and celery tops into pot and bring to a boil. Reduce heat to medium and simmer for one hour.
- ❈ Remove ribs from pot and cool slightly. Baste ribs with BBQ sauce on both sides.
- ❈ Preheat BBQ to medium high heat. Place ribs on BBQ and grill until brown and glazed with sauce, about 4 – 5 minutes a side.
- ❈ Makes 4 servings.

BBQ Sauce

2 tablespoons tomato paste

3 tablespoons vegetable oil

1 teaspoon balsamic vinegar

2 teaspoons Worcestershire sauce

1 teaspoon kitchen bouquet

½ teaspoon Mrs. Dash Extra Spicy

½ teaspoon dried thyme

1 teaspoon lime juice

1 teaspoon lemon juice

Nutrition Information Per Serving (BBQ Sauce)	
Calories	113.64
Protein	1.61 g.
Carbs	4.92 g.
Fat	11.32 g.

❀ Mix all ingredients together with a small whisk. Refrigerate for at least one hour before use. This makes enough sauce for 4 servings.

Spicy BBQ Sauce

2 tablespoons tomato paste

3 tablespoons vegetable oil

2 teaspoons Worcestershire sauce

1 teaspoon kitchen bouquet

½ teaspoon Mrs. Dash Extra Spicy

1 teaspoon dried thyme

1 teaspoon dried rosemary

1 teaspoon cayenne

2 teaspoons lime juice

1 teaspoon lemon juice

Nutrition Information Per Serving (Spicy Sauce)	
Calories	117.14
Protein	1.69 g.
Carbs	5.64 g.
Fat	11.40g.

❀ Mix all ingredients together with a small whisk. Refrigerate for at least one hour before use. This makes enough sauce for 4 servings.

Chili

1½ lbs. round ground

1 tablespoon olive oil

1 large sweet onion, minced

1 green pepper, minced

28 fl. oz. can diced tomatoes

10 fl. oz. can kidney beans

10½ oz. can tomato soup

1 teaspoon cayenne

salt & fresh ground pepper to taste

Nutrition Information Per Serving	
Calories	318.74
Protein	26.47 g.
Carbs	20.24 g.
Fat	14.12 g.

❀ Preheat oven to 350°.

❀ In heavy skillet, heat olive oil over medium heat and add round ground. Add salt and pepper to taste and cook, while stirring to break up the meat into bite sized pieces, until completely browned, approximately 5 minutes. Using slotted spoon remove the meat from the skillet and place in a 4 quart casserole.

❀ Place onions and green pepper in the skillet and sauté until soft, about 5 minutes. Using slotted spoon, remove from skillet and add to casserole.

❀ Add cayenne, tomatoes, kidney beans and tomato soup to casserole and stir until well mixed.

❀ Place casserole in oven and bake for at least one hour and up to three hours. If baking for more than 1 hour, reduce heat and stir every hour or so to combine and keep from sticking. This tastes better the longer it simmers.

❀ Makes 6 servings.

Note: This is high in carbs, even with reduced amounts of kidney beans, so I save it for days when the rest of my meal plan is very low. It is just too good to give up entirely.

Grilled Herb Steak

2 lbs. boneless, sirloin steak (1½" thick)

½ cup red wine

2 tablespoons olive oil

½ teaspoon dried rosemary

1 teaspoon dried thyme

1 teaspoon fresh ground pepper

½ teaspoon salt

Nutrition Information Per Serving	
Calories	375.05
Protein	28.47 g.
Carbs	0.88 g.
Fat	26.50 g.

❁ Place steak in a shallow dish. In a small bowl whisk together the olive oil, red wine, thyme, rosemary, salt and pepper. Pour over steak and turn to coat. Cover and refrigerate for 1-2 hours.

❁ Heat grill to medium high. Place steak on grill and close cover. Grill for 8 – 10 minutes a side for medium, depending on thickness of steak. Test for doneness by making a small cut in the center of the steak.

❁ Transfer steak to cutting board and tent with foil for 5 minutes. Slice thinly across the grain.

❁ Makes 6 – 8 servings.

Grilled Sirloin with Red Wine Sauce

2 lbs. sirloin steak, 1½" thick

2 tablespoons fresh ground pepper

1 teaspoon salt

2 tablespoons butter

½ cup chopped green onion

1 packet Splenda™

2 cloves garlic, minced

1 tablespoon fresh rosemary, minced

1 tablespoon fresh thyme, minced

1½ cups beef bouillon

¼ cup red wine

2 teaspoons cornstarch

Nutrition Information Per Serving	
Calories	278.39
Protein	21.59 g.
Carbs	1.85 g.
Fat	19.27 g.

※ Preheat grill to medium high. Dust steak with salt and pepper and rub into skin. Grill 8 – 9 minutes on each side for medium or until desired doneness. Test with small knife before removing from grill. Remove to carving board and tent with tin foil for 5 minutes.

※ While steak is grilling make sauce in saucepan on the stove. Heat the butter over medium heat and add onion. Sauté for approximately 5 minutes, until soft. Stir in Splenda™ and herbs and continue cooking for another minute.

※ Add beef bouillon and wine and bring mixture to a boil. Simmer for about 10 minutes until reduced by half. Add the cornstarch to a little water to dissolve, and then add to the wine sauce. Stir well to blend and cook for another 5 minutes.

※ Carve the steak on the diagonal into thin slices and pour wine sauce over the steak.

※ Makes 8 servings.

Grilled Tenderloin with Fresh Herb Salsa

4, 6 oz. tenderloin steaks, 1½" thick
1 tablespoon olive oil
1 tablespoon fresh ground pepper
salt to taste
4 slices bacon
kitchen string

Fresh Herb Salsa
½ bunch of fresh flat leaf parsley
(regular fresh parsley will do)
10 fresh basil leaves
10 fresh mint leaves
1 clove garlic, minced
1 tablespoon Dijon mustard
1 teaspoon red wine vinegar
⅓ cup olive oil
salt & fresh ground pepper to taste

Nutrition Information Per Serving	
Calories	370.57
Protein	14.02 g.
Carbs	1.53 g.
Fat	35.72 g.

- Wrap each steak with a piece of bacon and secure with kitchen string, making steaks uniform in size.
- Rub steaks with olive oil and pepper. Salt to taste.
- Grill over hot BBQ until desired doneness. (Generally 6 – 8 minutes per side for rare, 8 – 10 minutes for medium, or 10 – 12 minutes per side for well done.) The cooking time will vary with steak thickness.
- Place on a serving platter, cut off string and let sit for 3 – 4 minutes. Serve with a hefty dollop of Fresh Herb Salsa on each steak.
- Fresh Herb Salsa: Finely chop all herbs. Add vinegar, oil and garlic and mix in blender or food processor to emulsify.
- Add salt & pepper to taste and let stand at room temperature in a covered dish for 30 minutes to blend flavors.
- Makes 4 servings.

London Broil

1½ lbs. boneless, sirloin steak (1½" thick)

⅓ cup soy sauce

3 tablespoons Worcestershire sauce

2 cloves garlic, minced

1 teaspoon dried thyme

1 teaspoon fresh ground pepper

Nutrition Information Per Serving	
Calories	380.79
Protein	34.72 g.
Carbs	1.72 g.
Fat	24.56 g.

❃ Place steak in a shallow dish. In a small bowl whisk together the soy sauce, Worcestershire sauce, garlic, pepper and thyme. Pour over steak and turn to coat. Cover and refrigerate for 2 – 4 hours.

❃ Heat grill to medium high. Place steak on grill and close cover. Grill for 8 – 10 minutes a side for medium, depending on thickness of steak. Test for doneness by making a small cut in the center of the steak.

❃ Transfer steak to cutting board and tent with foil for 5 minutes. Slice thinly across the grain.

❃ Makes 4 – 6 servings.

Meat Loaf

1½ lbs. lean ground beef

1 celery stalk, diced

½ medium red onion, diced

2 small fresh mushrooms, diced

1 egg, slightly beaten

1 tablespoon fine bread crumbs

3 tablespoons undiluted beef consommé

1 teaspoon Fine Herbs

salt and freshly ground pepper to taste

Nutrition Information Per Serving	
Calories	251.34
Protein	23.05 g.
Carbs	4.26 g.
Fat	15.13 g.

- ❁ Preheat oven to 400°.
- ❁ Put meat in a large mixing bowl and add all other ingredients but beef consommé. Mix well with wooden spoon.
- ❁ Place in a loaf pan that has been sprayed with a no-stick agent. Press firmly into pan with spoon and smooth top. Spoon beef consommé on top of mixture.
- ❁ Bake for one hour.
- ❁ Makes 6 servings.

Meat Loaf with Tomato Sauce

1½ lbs. lean ground beef

1 celery stalk, diced

½ medium red onion, diced

2 small fresh mushrooms, diced

1 egg, slightly beaten

1 tablespoon fine bread crumbs

salt and freshly ground pepper to taste

Tomato Sauce

4 tablespoons tomato paste

1 tablespoon olive oil

2 tablespoons water

1 teaspoon Fine Herbs

Nutrition Information Per Serving	
Calories	237.28
Protein	22.51 g.
Carbs	4.10 g.
Fat	14.05 g.

- ❀ Preheat oven to 400°.
- ❀ Put meat in a large mixing bowl and add all other ingredients but tomato sauce. Mix well with wooden spoon.
- ❀ Place in a loaf pan that has been sprayed with a non-stick agent. Press firmly into pan with spoon and smooth top. Mix tomato paste, water and olive oil to make sauce and spoon over mixture. Sprinkle with Fine Herbs.
- ❀ Bake for one hour.
- ❀ Makes 6 servings.

Peppered Steak

1 steak, 2 – 3 lbs. (tenderloin, sirloin or New York strip, at least 1½" thick)

2 tablespoons olive oil

2 garlic cloves, finely minced

1½ teaspoons cracked pepper

½ teaspoon cayenne pepper

½ teaspoon dried thyme leaves

½ teaspoon dried oregano

Nutrition Information Per Serving	
Calories	362.35
Protein	28.47 g.
Carbs	0.73 g.
Fat	26.50 g.

- ❀ Preheat oven to 450°, or preheat grill to medium high.
- ❀ Brush both sides of the steak with the olive oil. Put the peppers, garlic and spices in a small bowl and mix to blend. Spread the mixture evenly on both sides of the steak and rub into the meat. Let stand for 20 minutes.
- ❀ If baking in the oven, bake for 5 minutes and reduce temperature to 375° and continue baking for another 25 – 30 minutes for medium or until desired doneness. Check for doneness before removing from oven.
- ❀ If grilling, cook on medium high grill turning occasionally for 18 – 20 minutes for medium or until desired doneness. Check for doneness before removing from grill.
- ❀ Place steak on cutting board and tent with foil for 5 minutes. Cut on the diagonal into thin slices.
- ❀ Makes 8 servings.

Quick Beef Hash

2 cups coarsely cut up left over beef, cut into bite sized pieces

1 cup fresh sliced mushrooms

1 cup diced red onion

2 tablespoons olive oil

salt & freshly ground pepper to taste

Nutrition Information Per Serving	
Calories	293.25
Protein	16.63 g.
Carbs	7.84 g.
Fat	22.38 g.

❀ Heat oil in frying pan over medium heat. Add all ingredients and seasonings. Cook, turning frequently, until onions and mushrooms are soft, about 5 – 6 minutes.

❀ Makes 2 servings.

Tip: This is a really good quick lunch, and can be made with leftover steak or roast beef.

Roast Beef with Wine Sauce

3 – 4 lb. prime rib roast (or any preferred cut)
2 tablespoons Dijon mustard
½ tablespoon olive oil
1 teaspoon each, dried rosemary & thyme
¼ teaspoon allspice

Red Wine Sauce
1 cup red wine
½ teaspoon cornstarch
¼ cup beef bouillon
1 teaspoon Dijon mustard
½ teaspoon soy sauce
1 tablespoon fresh chopped parsley
1 teaspoon fresh ground pepper

Nutrition Information Per Serving	
Calories	274.27
Protein	33.31 g.
Carbs	1.48 g.
Fat	12.57 g.

❧ In a small dish, whisk together Dijon mustard, oil and spices. Place roast in a roasting pan that has been treated with a no-stick agent. Brush roast with the mustard-herb preparation and let stand for 30 minutes at room temperature.

❧ Preheat oven to 350°. Place roast in oven and cook for approximately 25 – 30 minutes a pound for medium. Remove roast to a carving board and tent with foil and let rest for 5 minutes before carving.

❧ While roast is cooking, add beef bouillon and cornstarch in a small sauce pan and stir to dissolve cornstarch. Add all remaining ingredients and stir to blend well. Simmer for 5 – 6 minutes, while stirring constantly, until sauce is thickened. Reduce heat and keep warm until roast has been carved. Sauce may be poured over meat, or served in a serving dish.

❧ Makes 6 – 8 servings.

Steak with Roasted Vegetables

1½ lb. sirloin steak, about 2" thick

2 medium carrots

2 small rutabagas

1 medium zucchini

8 pearl onions or

1 medium sweet onion

4 tablespoons olive oil

fresh ground pepper and salt to taste

Nutrition Information Per Serving	
Calories	559.63
Protein	37.83 g.
Carbs	17.87 g.
Fat	42.86 g.

Dijon Steak Sauce

⅓ cup Dijon mustard

1 teaspoon fresh chopped mint

1 teaspoon fresh chopped thyme

- ❖ Preheat oven to 450°. Wash and peel carrots. Cut in half lengthwise, then into 1½" pieces. Wash and peel rutabagas and cut into 1½" pieces.
- ❖ If using medium sweet onion, peel and cut into 8ths. If using pearl onions, peel and wash.
- ❖ Wash zucchini and cut in half lengthways, and then into 2" pieces.
- ❖ Combine vegetables in a large bowl with 3 tablespoons of olive oil and toss to coat. Sprinkle with fresh ground pepper and salt.
- ❖ Spray a large baking pan with no stick product and spoon vegetables into pan.
- ❖ Roast vegetables for 30 – 40 minutes or until cooked to desired softness, stirring regularly to brown evenly on all sides.

continued next page

Steak with Roasted Vegetables cont.

❀ Brush steak with remaining tablespoon of olive oil. Coat generously with fresh ground pepper and salt. Place steak on a separate small roasting pan that has been prepared with no stick product.

❀ Roast steak until desired doneness, about 30 minutes for medium. Test for doneness by making a small incision in the center of the steak.

❀ Remove from oven and let stand under a tent of foil for 3 – 5 minutes. Cut steak into thin strips on the diagonal.

❀ Mix mustard with the fresh herbs to make sauce. Let stand for at least 30 minutes to allow flavors to blend.

❀ Serve thinly sliced steak with roasted vegetables and a dollop of mustard sauce.

❀ Makes 4-6 servings.

Note: Nutrition was calculated based on only 4 servings. The carbohydrates are slightly higher than other recipes, but your full meal is calculated, including vegetables. Reduce the carbohydrates by reducing the amount of mustard sauce, or the carrots.

Teriyaki Burgers

1 lb. lean ground beef

¼ cup soy sauce

¼ cup minced red onion

½ teaspoon grated fresh ginger
(¼ teaspoon dried ginger)

1 clove garlic, minced

½ teaspoon ground cumin

freshly ground pepper to taste

Nutrition Information Per Serving	
Calories	336.59
Protein	34.27 g.
Carbs	1.89 g.
Fat	20.16 g.

- ❖ Combine soy sauce, onions, garlic, ginger and pepper in a small bowl.
- ❖ Add soy mixture to beef and mix thoroughly.
- ❖ Divide into four portions and form patties.
- ❖ Preheat grill to medium high heat and cook 4 – 5 minutes a side depending on the thickness of the patty.
- ❖ Makes 4 servings.

Lamb Chops with Herbs

¼ cup white wine vinegar

1 tablespoon fresh chopped rosemary

1 tablespoon fresh chopped thyme

1 clove garlic, minced

1 tablespoon olive oil

salt & fresh ground pepper to taste

8 loin lamb chops

Nutrition Information Per Serving	
Calories	225.18
Protein	27.31 g.
Carbs	1.11 g.
Fat	11.34 g.

❖ In a shallow bowl, mix all ingredients except the lamb chops. Add chops and let stand at room temperature for 5 – 10 minutes, turning to coat.

❖ Preheat grill to medium high heat. Place chops on the BBQ and grill, turning once, for approximately 12 – 16 minutes for medium well chops. Check for doneness before removing from grill.

Tip: This marinade is also good with pork chops or chicken breasts.

Rack of Lamb with Herbs and Spices

2 racks of lamb (1½ – 2 lbs.)

1 tablespoon olive oil

1½ tablespoons Dijon mustard

1 teaspoon dried rosemary

1 teaspoon Fine Herbs

salt and freshly ground pepper to taste

Nutrition Information Per Serving	
Calories	426.29
Protein	21.14 g.
Carbs	2.46 g.
Fat	35.66 g.

❧ Preheat oven to 450°. Spray roasting rack and large roasting pan with no-stick spray. Pat racks of lamb dry.

❧ Heat the olive oil in a large frying pan. Brown the racks of lamb on all sides, about 2 – 3 minutes a side. May have to brown racks one at a time depending on size, and may need to add additional olive oil if browning separately.

❧ Remove lamb to a rack in a roasting pan. Brush lamb with mustard on both sides and sprinkle with rosemary, Fine Herbs, salt and pepper.

❧ Roast at 450° for about 15 – 20 minutes for medium or until desired doneness. Roasting time will vary with thickness of rack. Check doneness by making small cut into meat to test.

❧ Transfer meat to serving platter and tent with foil and let stand for 5 minutes. Cut racks into two servings each and garnish with sprigs of fresh rosemary. Serve with herb sauce.

❧ Makes 4 servings.

continued next page

Rack of Lamb with Herbs and Spices cont.

Herb Sauce

1 teaspoon each olive oil & butter

1 clove garlic, finely minced

1 tablespoon finely minced green onion

½ teaspoon dried thyme

½ teaspoon dried rosemary

2 tablespoons Dijon mustard

2 tablespoons grainy Dijon mustard

¼ cup chicken bouillon

- In small saucepan, over medium low heat, melt butter and olive oil.
- Add garlic and onion and sauté 3 – 4 minutes until soft. Add the thyme, rosemary and Fine Herbs and the chicken bouillon.
- Bring to a boil and reduce by half, stirring constantly. This will take 4 – 5 minutes.
- Remove from heat and stir in mustards. Cool and refrigerate until ready to use. May be made the day before, and kept in the fridge.

Lemon Herb Lamb Chops

8 lean lamb chops, about 1½" thick

zest and juice of 1 medium lemon

2 tablespoons white wine

1 tablespoon olive oil

2 garlic cloves, minced

1 tablespoon each, fresh chopped thyme, parsley, and mint

1 teaspoon fresh ground pepper

½ teaspoon salt

Nutrition Information Per Serving	
Calories	293.06
Protein	20.78 g.
Carbs	2.21 g.
Fat	21.45 g.

❀ In a small bowl, whisk together oil, lemon zest and juice, white wine and fresh herbs. Place chops in a shallow dish and pour marinade over them, turning to coat. Let stand 1 hour at room temperature.

❀ Preheat oven broiler. Spray broiler rack with no stick agent, and place chops on rack. Place rack in oven, about 6" from broiler. Broil for approximately 7 – 8 minutes on each side until well browned for medium to well done chops. Doneness will vary with thickness, always test before removing from oven.

❀ Makes 4 servings.

Note: These chops may also be grilled on a medium high grill, for approximately the same amount of time.

Grilled Dijon Pork Chops

4 loin pork chops, 1½" thick & bone in

4 tablespoons Dijon mustard

6 teaspoons olive oil

1 clove garlic, minced

½ teaspoon dried rosemary

1 teaspoon dried thyme

1 teaspoon fresh ground pepper

½ teaspoon salt

Nutrition Information Per Serving	
Calories	389.11
Protein	23.26 g.
Carbs	0.46 g.
Fat	32.78 g.

❊ Combine mustard, olive oil, herbs and salt and pepper in a small bowl. Pour mixture over chops in a shallow bowl and turn to coat. Let stand for 15 – 20 minutes.

❊ Preheat grill to medium high. Add the pork chops, close the lid and grill, turning once, for 5 – 6 minutes a side or until juice runs clear and meat is cooked through. Test for doneness before removing from grill.

❊ Makes 4 servings.

Grilled Herb Pork Chops

4 loin pork chops
(about 1½ lbs. with bone in)

¼ cup white wine

½ cup fresh lemon juice

¼ olive oil

2 tablespoons fresh parsley, chopped

2 tablespoons fresh rosemary, chopped

2 tablespoons finely minced onion

1 tablespoon fresh ground pepper

Nutrition Information Per Serving	
Calories	348.74
Protein	23.46 g.
Carbs	3.59 g.
Fat	25.48 g.

❀ Combine all ingredients in a shallow pan. Add pork chops and turn to coat. Let stand for half an hour to an hour in the fridge.

❀ Preheat grill to medium heat. Add chops and grill for 5 – 6 minutes a side depending on thickness. Check doneness by making small cut in the middle of the chop.

❀ Makes 4 servings.

Pork Loin in White Wine

4 boneless loin chops (1 lb.)

1 teaspoon fresh ground pepper

1 tablespoon olive oil

1 tablespoon fresh chopped rosemary

½ cup chicken bouillon

1 cup fresh mushrooms, sliced

½ cup white wine

1 teaspoon lime zest

1 tablespoon lime juice

1 teaspoon cornstarch

1 tablespoon fresh chopped parsley

1 clove garlic , minced

Nutrition Information Per Serving	
Calories	270.13
Protein	23.88 g.
Carbs	2.64 g.
Fat	15.55 g.

- Heat oil in frying pan over medium heat. Grind pepper over chops and press in. Brown chops in oil, 2 – 3 minutes a side. Transfer to oven proof pan and put in a warm oven (300°).
- Add garlic and mushrooms to pan and sauté for 3 – 4 minutes until soft. Add bouillon, wine, lime zest, juice and fresh rosemary to pan and bring to a boil. If the sauce is a bit thin, dissolve the cornstarch in a little water and add it to the mixture.
- Add chops back to the pan and simmer over medium heat, turning to coat for 3 – 4 minutes. Serve chops with sauce and a sprinkle of fresh parsley.
- Makes 4 servings.

Pork Medallions with Cream Sauce

1½ lbs. pork tenderloin

1 tablespoon butter

1 tablespoon olive oil

3 green onions, chopped

1 cup fresh sliced mushrooms

½ cup heavy cream

½ cup chicken bouillon

1 tablespoon white wine

½ teaspoon cornstarch

salt and freshly ground pepper to taste

Nutrition Information Per Serving	
Calories	409.42
Protein	35.28 g.
Carbs	3.05 g.
Fat	27.60 g.

- ❀ Cut pork tenderloin cross wise into 1" thick medallions. Sprinkle with salt and freshly ground pepper.
- ❀ Heat butter and olive oil in heavy frying pan over medium high heat.
- ❀ Working in batches, sauté medallions until browned on both sides and cooked through, about 4 minutes a side.
- ❀ Transfer medallions to oven proof dish, tent with foil and place in a warm oven (about 250°).
- ❀ Add mushrooms and green onion to pan and sauté until soft, about 3 minutes.
- ❀ Add cream, chicken bouillon and wine. Bring mixture to a boil and lower heat. Cook, stirring constantly, until thick enough to coat spoon. You may need to add the cornstarch to help thicken. If cornstarch is needed, dissolve in a small amount of water before adding to the sauce.
- ❀ Season sauce with freshly ground pepper and salt. Return the medallions to the pan and continue cooking for 2 minutes while stirring constantly to coat.
- ❀ Divide warm medallions onto four plates, and cover with sauce.
- ❀ Makes 4 servings.

Savory Pork Chops with Gravy

4 loin pork chops, 1½" thick & bone in

2 teaspoons flour

1 tablespoon olive oil

¾ teaspoon dried oregano

¾ teaspoon dried rosemary

1 teaspoon fresh ground pepper

½ teaspoon salt

1 small onion, thinly sliced and separated into rings

1 cup chicken bouillon

Nutrition Information Per Serving	
Calories	247.43
Protein	23.58 g.
Carbs	2.70 g.
Fat	15.36 g.

- Combine herbs and salt and pepper in a small bowl. Sprinkle herbs over chops and press in with hands.
- In a large no-stick fry pan, heat oil over medium high heat. Brown chops in oil, for 3 – 5 minutes on each side, until golden. Remove chops to oven proof dish and place in a warm oven, approximately 300°.
- Place onion in frying pan and cook for 3 – 4 minutes until golden. Add the flour, stirring constantly until well blended. Add the chicken bouillon stirring constantly and reduce heat to medium. Bring to a boil and continue cooking until mixture is reduced by half.
- Add the pork chops and any liquid in the pan back to the frying pan and turn to coat. Simmer for 2 – 3 minutes.
- Makes 4 servings.

Tenderloin of Pork with White Wine

1½ lbs. boneless loin of pork

2 cloves garlic, quartered

8 slices bacon

2 tablespoons olive oil

1 large onion, cut into 8ths lengthways

8 large mushrooms

1 cup chicken bouillon

2 sprigs fresh thyme

2 sprigs fresh rosemary

1 bay leaf

½ cup white wine

salt & fresh ground pepper

Nutrition Information Per Serving	
Calories	565.58
Protein	39.76 g.
Carbs	5.70 g.
Fat	39.54 g.

❀ Preheat oven to 350°.

❀ With sharp knife, make small openings in the pork loin and insert garlic. Season pork with salt and freshly ground pepper. Wrap each tenderloin in bacon lengthways. Tie with kitchen string in 2 or 3 places to secure the bacon.

❀ Heat the oil until hot in a 2 quart casserole. Add the pork and sauté until golden brown on all sides, about 6 – 7 minutes. Remove and set aside.

❀ Add onions and mushrooms and sauté until golden. Return the meat to the casserole. Add chicken bouillon, thyme, rosemary and bay leaf and bring to a boil over medium heat.

❀ Cover and place in the oven for 1½ hours. Add the white wine to the casserole 30 minutes before serving, and return to the oven.

❀ Remove the casserole from the oven. Remove the pork tenderloins and cut off the kitchen string. Cut into slices, using a sharp knife to make diagonal cuts. Serve with onion, mushrooms and a little sauce.

❀ Makes 4 servings.

DESSERTS

Cherry Compote

⅔ cup red wine

1½ pounds of fresh cherries

4 packets Splenda™

½ teaspoon cinnamon

2 teaspoons cornstarch

Nutrition Information Per Serving	
Calories	22.86
Protein	0.11 g.
Carbs	2.38 g.
Fat	0.08 g.

❁ Wash and pit cherries. Set aside.

❁ Put red wine, cinnamon and Splenda™ in a saucepan and heat over low heat 2 – 3 minutes until Splenda™ dissolves.

❁ Add the cherries and simmer for 6 – 8 minutes. Add some water if the wine does not cover the fruit. Remove from heat after 8 minutes.

❁ Dissolve cornstarch in a little water and add to the cherry mixture. Return to medium heat and bring to a boil, stirring constantly. The sauce will thicken into a syrup-like consistency.

❁ Transfer to a serving bowl, or individual dessert bowls.

❁ May be served warm or cold.

❁ Makes 8 servings.

Note: This is wonderful over a small dish of no sugar added vanilla ice cream, if you can afford the additional carbohydrates.

Chocolate Indulgence

5 oz unsweetened chocolate

5 oz semi-sweet chocolate

1 cup unsalted butter

6 eggs

5 packets Splenda™

1 tablespoon brandy extract

1 tablespoon flour

To Finish

1 cup heavy cream

4 packets Splenda™

sprigs of fresh mint

1 cup fresh strawberries or raspberries

Nutrition Information Per Serving	
Calories	343.50
Protein	5.08 g.
Carbs	13.88 g.
Fat	32.79 g.

✿ Preheat oven to 350°. Grease a 9" x 2" round spring form pan. Cut parchment paper for bottom and grease paper. Wrap bottom and up the sides of pan in tinfoil to ensure it is completely water tight.

✿ In top of double boiler, melt chocolate and butter. This will be quicker if chocolate and butter are chopped into pieces. Add Splenda™ and stir until smooth. Remove from heat and let cool 2 – 3 minutes. Set the top of the double boiler on a tea towel to absorb any moisture.

✿ Beat eggs in a large bowl with electric beater for 1 minute. Add brandy extract and sifted flour and beat just to blend.

✿ Gradually add chocolate mixture to egg mixture, beating slowly until completely blended. Pour into spring form pan.

✿ Place spring form pan in a roasting pan that has ½" of water in the bottom. Place in the center of the oven and bake for 25 – 30 minutes, until the edges are set and the center is still soft. *continued next page*

Chocolate Indulgence cont.

※ Remove from the oven. Gently remove tin foil from around pan and place on a wire rack to cool for 15 minutes. The cake may sink in the center and may even crack but do not be alarmed.

※ Remove the cake from spring form pan, then place cake top down on wire rack to remove parchment paper. Let cool completely. You may decide that the bottom now becomes the top of the cake. I just pick whichever has the most pleasing appearance. This is a dense, heavy cake that is not very high.

※ Move cake to a serving plate. Garnish with a light dusting of unsweetened cocoa, using a sifter to dust.

To Finish

※ Slice a thin wedge of cake. Serve with a dollop of heavy cream that has been whipped with Splenda™, a sprig of fresh mint and 2 or 3 fresh berries.

※ Makes 10 servings.

Chocolate Pavé

6 oz unsweetened chocolate

4 oz semisweet chocolate

½ cup unsalted butter

6 egg yolks

4 tablespoons heavy cream

4 packets Splenda™

To Finish

½ cup heavy cream

2 packets Splenda™

16-24 fresh cherries or raspberries

Nutrition Information Per Serving	
Calories	369.00
Protein	5.13 g.
Carbs	15.81 g.
Fat	35.76 g.

- Line a mini-loaf pan (2 cup) with two strips of wax paper – one for the length and one for the width of the pan. Allow at least ½" to overhang on all sides. Set aside.

- In the top of a double boiler, melt the chocolate and butter. Add 4 packets of Splenda™ and stir until smooth. Set aside on a tea towel to cool for 2-3 minutes.

- In a large bowl, use a whisk to beat together egg yolks and the 4 tablespoons of heavy cream until smooth and creamy. Beat 2 or 3 spoonfuls of the chocolate mixture into the egg mixture.

- Gradually whisk the rest of the chocolate mixture into the egg mixture until completely blended.

- Pour into the wax paper lined loaf pan and let cool to room temperature. Place in the fridge for at least 3 hours.

- Remove the pavé by inverting loaf pan. Peel off wax paper and place on serving dish.

To Serve

- Cut thin slices of the pavé and serve with a dollop of cream whipped with the Splenda™ and 2-3 fresh cherries or raspberries.

- Makes 8 servings.

Coconut Macaroons

1 egg, beaten

4 packets Splenda™

2 cups shredded, sweetened coconut

½ teaspoon vanilla extract

¼ cup heavy cream

Nutrition Information Per Serving	
Calories	57.07
Protein	0.79 g.
Carbs	3.72 g.
Fat	4.17 g.

※ Put beaten egg into heavy mixing bowl. Add Splenda™ and mix with a fork. Add vanilla extract and coconut. Finally add the heavy cream and blend well.

※ Using a tablespoon of batter, mound into 1" high mounds on a greased cookie sheet, or a sheet lined with parchment or a "sil" baking pad.

※ Bake at 325° until golden brown, about 10 – 12 minutes.

※ Remove from oven and leave on the cookie sheet for a couple of minutes to cool, then remove to a cake rack to continue cooling.

※ Makes 18 cookies.

Crème Framboise (Raspberry Cream)

2½ cups heavy cream

4 egg yolks

6 packets Splenda™

1 teaspoon vanilla

1 cup fresh raspberries
(or frozen unsweetened)

Nutrition Information Per Serving	
Calories	397.59
Protein	4.07 g.
Carbs	6.42 g.
Fat	40.22 g.

❀ Preheat oven to 300°. Combine the egg yolks, Splenda™ and vanilla in a separate bowl and beat with electric mixer for 2 minutes. Set aside.

❀ Wash and pat dry the raspberries and set aside.

❀ Put cream in top of double boiler over medium heat, and stirring constantly bring the cream to just below a boil. (The water in the bottom of the double boiler should be boiling lightly.) This will take about 5 minutes and you will know that it is ready when it starts to froth lightly.

❀ Add a small amount of the hot cream (2 – 3 teaspoons) into the egg mixture and stir to temper the egg. Add the rest of the cream and stir to blend.

❀ Divide the custard evenly into 6 individual ramekins. Evenly divide the raspberries among the ramekins and gently drop into the custard. I like to try to place at least one raspberry so that it sits on top of the custard to add color. (If using frozen berries, they must be thawed before using.)

continued next page

Crème Framboise (Raspberry Cream) cont.

❀ Pour ½" of water in the bottom of a large roasting pan. Gently place the ramekins into the roasting pan, ensuring that no water gets into the custard.

❀ Bake for 35 – 40 minutes until the custard is set in the middle and the edges are starting to brown.

❀ Cool and refrigerate until serving.

❀ Makes 6 servings.

Note: This is a lovely creamy dessert, and the raspberries add a surprising taste treat.

French Cream

	Nutrition Information Per Serving	
2½ cups heavy cream	Calories	387.54
4 egg yolks	Protein	3.89 g.
6 packets Splenda™	Carbs	4.05 g.
1 teaspoon vanilla	Fat	40.11 g.

- ✤ Preheat oven to 300°.
- ✤ Put cream in top of double boiler over medium high heat and while stirring constantly, bring the cream to just below boiling. This will take about 5 minutes and you will know it is ready when it starts to froth lightly.
- ✤ Put the egg yolks, Splenda™ and vanilla extract in a mixing bowl and beat with electric mixer for 2 – 3 minutes.
- ✤ Slowly add 2 – 3 tablespoons of the hot cream to the yolk mixture to temper it, then add the rest of the cream mixture and stir to combine.
- ✤ Pour the mixture into a shallow baking dish and place it in a roasting pan that is half full of water. Bake at 300° for 45 – 60 minutes or until set. (edges will be brown)
- ✤ Cool and refrigerate until ready to serve.
- ✤ Serve with garnish of fresh berries.
- ✤ Makes 6 servings.

Individual Chocolate Cakes

6 oz. bittersweet chocolate

½ cup butter

4 eggs

2 tablespoons prepared strong coffee

10 packets Splenda™, divided

2 tablespoons flour

½ cup heavy cream

6 sprigs fresh mint

Nutrition Information Per Serving	
Calories	338.65
Protein	5.96 g.
Carbs	18.90 g.
Fat	26.70 g.

- ❂ Preheat oven to 400°.
- ❂ Spray 6 individual ramekins with no-stick agent.
- ❂ Melt chocolate and butter in the top of a double boiler and stir to blend. Set aside.
- ❂ Beat eggs with coffee until foamy. Gradually add 8 packets of Splenda™, one packet at a time, and continue beating until light and fluffy.
- ❂ Add flour and chocolate and beat at low speed until just blended.
- ❂ Fill each ramekin ¾ full with cake batter and place the ramekins on a cookie sheet.
- ❂ Bake for 12 – 15 minutes until cakes are raised and a crust has formed over the top. Cool for at least 10 minutes.
- ❂ Whip the heavy cream with the 2 packets of Splenda™, until stiff peaks form.
- ❂ Invert cakes onto individual dessert plates and garnish with a dollop of whipped cream and a sprig of fresh mint. These are best if served warm, but may also be served at room temperature.
- ❂ Makes 6 servings.

Tip: These are lovely with a bit of Raspberry Puree placed on the bottom of the plate, as additional garnish. The carbohydrate count on these is high, so I save them for special occasions, and watch the content of the other dishes in the meal.

Marinated Pineapple & Cherries

2 cups water

zest & juice of 1 lime

4 packets Splenda™

½ teaspoon cinnamon

¼ cup sherry

½ pineapple

½ – ¾ lb. fresh cherries

Nutrition Information Per Serving	
Calories	149.97
Protein	1.09 g.
Carbs	10.62 g.
Fat	11.42 g.

To Finish

1 cup of heavy cream

2 packets Splenda™

sprigs of fresh mint

❀ Put water, lime juice and zest, Splenda™, cinnamon and sherry in a heavy saucepan and bring to a simmer over medium heat. Reduce to a syrup-like consistency by simmering for approximately 30 minutes. Remove from heat and cool 15 minutes.

❀ Cut off outer skin and hard center core of pineapple, and cut fruit into bite sized pieces. Put pineapple chunks into large bowl. Add cherries that have been washed and pitted (approximately 1 cup).

❀ Strain cooled marinade and pour over fruit. Put in the fridge for 2 – 3 hours, stirring occasionally.

❀ Whip the cream while gradually adding the Splenda™ until stiff peaks form.

❀ Spoon the fruit into individual dessert dishes. Finish with a dollop of whipped cream and a sprig of fresh mint.

❀ Makes 8 servings.

Peach Delight

½ cup fresh or frozen unsweetened raspberries

4 packets Splenda™, divided

2 fresh peaches, peeled, pitted and quartered

½ cup heavy cream

Nutrition Information Per Serving	
Calories	145.93
Protein	1.24 g.
Carbs	11.62 g.
Fat	11.16 g.

※ Whip the heavy cream with 2 packets of Splenda™ and set aside.

※ Process the raspberries in a food processor with 2 packets of Splenda™ until smooth.

※ Place the peach quarters on a broiler pan sprayed with a no stick agent and place under a hot broiler until just brown, 2 – 3 minutes.

※ Place two peach quarters in a dessert dish and drizzle with a generous portion of raspberry puree. Garnish with a dollop of whipped cream.

※ Makes 4 servings.

Quick & Easy Mousse

1 small (1 oz.)sugar free JELL-O®
instant pudding mix
or (28 gram) package of Light JELL-O®
instant pudding mix

1½ cups skim milk

½ cup of heavy cream

Nutrition Information Per Serving	
Calories	154.73
Protein	3.74 g.
Carbs	10.29 g.
Fat	11.17 g.

❊ In a bowl, combine the pudding mix, skim milk and heavy cream.
  Beat with an electric mixer for 2 minutes until thickened.

❊ Pour or spoon into individual dessert dishes and refrigerate for at
  least 20 minutes, until set.

❊ Makes 4 servings.

*Tip: This quick and easy dessert may be made using any flavor JELL-O®
instant pudding mix. The grams of carbohydrate will vary slightly with the
flavor of pudding. Vanilla pudding mix was used for the purpose of
determining the nutritional information.*

Rhubarb & Strawberry Supreme

3 cups fresh rhubarb, cut into 1" pieces

2 cups fresh strawberries, cut into halves
or quarters

⅓ cup of water

4 packets of Splenda™

1 teaspoon lemon juice

To Finish

1 cup of heavy cream

2 packets of Splenda™

½ cup toasted almond slivers

Nutrition Information Per Serving	
Calories	169.24
Protein	2.76 g.
Carbs	7.63 g.
Fat	14.99 g.

❀ Put water, rhubarb and Splenda™ into sauce pan and heat over medium heat until water simmers. Lower heat and simmer for 5 minutes. Add strawberry pieces and continue to simmer for 2 – 3 additional minutes. Remove from heat and let cool.

❀ To serve, whip the cream with Splenda™ until stiff peaks form. Place rhubarb & strawberry mixture in individual dessert dishes, garnish with a dollop of whipped cream and a sprinkle of toasted almond slivers.

❀ Makes 8 servings.

Strawberries Dipped in Chocolate

12 medium strawberries

2 oz. unsweetened chocolate

8 packets Splenda™

¼ teaspoon heavy cream

Nutrition Information Per Serving	
Calories	31.29
Protein	0.56 g.
Carbs	2.85 g.
Fat	2.70 g.

✿ Wash and pat dry strawberries, leaving stems intact. Set aside.

✿ Melt chocolate in the top of a double boiler. Stir until smooth. Add the Splenda™ and continue stirring until dissolved. Add the heavy cream, stirring constantly. Remove top of double boiler from the heat and set on a kitchen towel.

✿ Holding berry by the green stem, dip it on both sides into the chocolate. You may want to scrap any excess off one side, on the side of the double boiler.

✿ Set the berry down on a small cookie sheet covered with wax paper. When all the berries have been dipped, put the cookie sheet in the fridge to set the chocolate. Berries should stay in the fridge until ready to serve.

✿ These can be prepared a half day ahead, but the berry will start to shrink inside the chocolate coating after a day.

✿ Makes 12 servings.

Note: You will need sweet, ripe berries for this treat. The chocolate is like a dark bittersweet coating.

Strawberry Mousse

1 small (8.5 g.) package of Strawberry
sugar free JELL-O® or Light JELL-O®

⅔ cup of boiling water

1 cup of ice cubes

1 cup of heavy cream

2 packets Splenda™

1 cup of finely cut up fresh strawberries

Nutrition Information Per Serving	
Calories	147.73
Protein	1.15 g.
Carbs	3.38 g.
Fat	14.78 g.

※ Whip the heavy cream with the Splenda™ until fairly stiff, and set aside.

※ In a large bowl, dissolve the JELL-O® powder in the boiling water and stir for 2 minutes until completely dissolved. Add the ice cubes and stir until the mixture begins to thicken, approximately 2 – 3 minutes. Remove any remaining un-melted ice cubes.

※ Add the whipped cream and whisk gently to combine. Fold in the fruit.

※ Spoon into individual dessert dishes and refrigerate for at least 30 minutes until set.

※ Makes 6 servings.

Tip: A similar dessert may be made using Raspberry JELL-O® and fresh fruit.

Strawberry Rhubarb Crumble

Filling

1 cup of ¼" pieces of fresh rhubarb

1 cup cut up fresh strawberries (4 large or 8 medium berries)

2 packets Splenda™

Topping

¼ cup rolled oats – not the instant variety

¼ cup finely chopped pecans

¾ tablespoon butter at room temperature

2 packets Splenda™

Nutrition Information Per Serving	
Calories	129.48
Protein	2.77 g.
Carbs	13.12 g.
Fat	8.08 g.

To Finish

½ cup of heavy cream

2 packets of Splenda™

fresh mint sprigs

- Mix together filling ingredients in a bowl and set aside. Mix together topping ingredients until crumbly mixture forms.
- Preheat oven to 375°. Grease 4 small individual ramekins. Divide fruit mixture equally among ramekins. Sprinkle oat and nut mixture evenly on top of fruit, covering as much of the fruit as possible. Place ramekins on cookie sheet and bake for 25 minutes or until tops are browned and fruit is bubbling.
- Cool at least 30 minutes before serving. Garnish with a dollop of whipped cream and a sprig of fresh mint.
- Makes 4 servings.

Stewed Rhubarb

3 cups fresh rhubarb, cut into 1" pieces

¼ cup of water

4 packets of Splenda™

1 teaspoon lemon juice

To Finish

½ cup of heavy cream

2 packets of Splenda™

fresh mint sprigs

Nutrition Information Per Serving	
Calories	31.29
Protein	0.56 g.
Carbs	2.85 g.
Fat	2.70 g.

❁ Put water, lemon juice, rhubarb and Splenda™ into sauce pan and heat over medium heat until water simmers. Lower heat and simmer for 10 minutes. Remove from heat and let cool.

❁ To serve, whip the cream with Splenda™ until stiff peaks form. Place rhubarb in individual dessert dishes, garnish with a dollop of whipped cream and a sprig of fresh mint.

❁ Makes 4 servings.

Note: If you are feeling indulgent, this is a wonderful topping for a light vanilla ice cream. Check the label to make sure you get the lowest carbohydrate content possible. No need for the whipped cream in this case.

Warm Chocolate Cakes

4 oz. bittersweet chocolate

½ cup butter, roughly chopped

2 large eggs

2 egg yolks

4 packets Splenda™

2 tablespoons flour

Nutrition Information Per Serving	
Calories	341.94
Protein	5.29 g.
Carbs	10.81 g.
Fat	34.46 g.

To Finish

Raspberry Puree & Whipped Cream
(see next page)

- ❀ Preheat oven to 350°. Butter 6 individual ramekins or custard cups.
- ❀ Put chocolate and butter pieces in the top of a double boiler with hot water in the bottom, over medium heat. Stir until melted and well blended. Remove from heat and cool.
- ❀ Using electric mixer, beat eggs, egg yolks and Splenda™ until thick and pale yellow, about 5 minutes.
- ❀ Fold cooled chocolate into egg mixture. Sift flour into chocolate and fold until just blended.
- ❀ Divide the mixture evenly among the prepared dishes and place them on a cookie sheet. Bake until the edges are set, but cakes are still soft in the middle, approximately 15 – 18 minutes.
- ❀ Serve warm with a drizzle of raspberry puree and a dollop of whipped cream.
- ❀ Makes 6 servings.

Raspberry Puree

½ cup fresh or frozen unsweetened
raspberries

2 packets of Splenda™

❧ Thaw berries, if frozen. Blend berries with Splenda™ in a food
processor until smooth. You may sift the puree if you do not like the
seeds or leave them, if desired.

*Note: There are many easy uses for this puree. It is nice with any chocolate
dessert, or drizzled over one of the vanilla or other mousse desserts.*

Whipped Cream

½ cup heavy cream

2 packets of Splenda™

❧ Beat the heavy cream with the Splenda™, until stiff peaks form.

Warm Spicy Peaches

2 tablespoons of butter

2 packets Splenda™

1 teaspoon vanilla extract

¼ teaspoon ground cardamom

¼ teaspoon ground nutmeg

4 ripe medium peaches

To Finish

½ cup heavy cream

2 packets Splenda™

Nutrition Information Per Serving	
Calories	90.92
Protein	0.64 g.
Carbs	9.56 g.
Fat	5.88 g.

- Clean, skin and pit peaches. Cut into ¼" thick slices and set aside.
- Melt butter in large frying pan over medium heat. Add Splenda™ and stir until dissolved. Add spices and stir for a minute or two.
- Add peaches and stir for approximately 5 minutes, turning occasionally to coat all sides.
- Whip heavy cream with the Splenda™, until stiff peaks form.
- Serve peaches in individual dessert dishes with a dollop of whipped cream on top.
- Makes 4 servings.

Tip: The peaches may be prepared earlier, up to a couple of hours before the meal, and gently reheated just before serving. They are best if served just warm, with the cool whipped cream.

White Chocolate Mousse

1 small (1 oz.) package of sugar free instant White Chocolate JELL-O® pudding mix

1½ cups of skim milk

1 cup + ½ cup heavy cream

2 packets Splenda™

Fresh strawberries or raspberries to garnish

Nutrition Information Per Serving	
Calories	236
Protein	3.72 g.
Carbs	6.41 g.
Fat	22.27 g.

- ❀ Whip 1 cup of the heavy cream with the Splenda™ until stiff peaks form.
- ❀ In another bowl, add JELL-O® powder, milk and remaining heavy cream and whisk by hand for 2 – 3 minutes until pudding starts to thicken.
- ❀ Add the whipped cream and whisk gently until well blended. Spoon into individual dessert dishes and place in the fridge for 25 – 30 minutes.
- ❀ Garnish with fresh fruit cut into thin slices and placed on top of mousse.
- ❀ Makes 6 servings.

ISBN 155369376-0

9 781553 693765